MW00953381

CHRONICLES OF A PARKY

CHRONICLES OF A PARKY

A Lighter Look
at a
Shaky Existence

RYAN OEVERMANN

Foreword by: Dr. Melissa Paquette

First Published in 2024 by Ryan Oevermann

Author:

Ryan Oevermann

Title:

Chronicles of a Parky: A Lighter Look at a Shaky Existence

ISBN : 9798332702914

Editor-in-chief: Ryan Oevermann

Cover design: Sue Oevermann & Derek Strokon

Cover & About the Author Photos: Lipsett Photography Group

Disclaimer:

The material in this publication is of anecdotal nature and general sharing but is not intended to provide specific guidance for particular circumstances and should not be relied on as a basis for any decision to take action or not to take action on any particular matter it covers. Readers should follow the advice of their physician, neurologist, or other medical professional where appropriate. To the maximum extent permitted by law, the author and publisher disclaim all responsibility and liability to any person, arising directly or indirectly from any person taking or not taking action based on the information in this publication.

DEDICATION

To my favourite people in the world, Sue, Landon and Tana. Thank you for enduring this with me, for always supporting me, never judging me, and of course, always loving me. Creating this life together has been by far my greatest achievement and I wouldn't trade it for anything.

To my wife specifically, I cannot say enough to match what you deserve. There are struggles and journeys that you have endured in my wake that others, including me, may never know about. This book is as much your victory as it is mine. Thank you and I love you.

TABLE OF CONTENTS

ENDORSEMENTS

"Who is cutting onions here? You never cease to amaze me Ryan... such inspiration needs to be shared widely!"
> -Jean-Yves Duret, VP, Electronic Arts

"Thank you for sharing your story. I've always seen you, across many years as one who will not shy away from a challenge and one who will use your time to help others. You have a wonderful and strong family beside you!! Keep strong as you have always been, sir!"
> -B. Beattie, GM/Chef Ship to Shore

"Ryan my friend, truly you are a remarkable man to shoulder this pod and to keep your spirits, your charisma and your bright outlook. Few could persevere like you have and will. You are a role model for everyone, demonstrating moral code, perseverance, discipline, integrity and still having time for compassion and caring for those around you. You are a hero!!! You are a man to admire!!!! You are a husband/father of the highest calibre and you have all of our love and admiration. Big hugs to you, Sue, and the kids!"
> -Master Kurt Ottesen, VII Dan ITF Taekwon-do

"I started reading this stunned and have ended full of hope. The optimism shines through."
> -Duane De Vries, Friend

"Ryan, not only are you an inspiration, you are one hell of a writer!"

-Paul Dickson, Canadian Conquistador

"An inspiration to us all. Thanks for staying optimistic as difficult as it can be sometimes. An engaging read as always. Thanks for sharing and being so open about your struggles and how you choose to go about dancing with them!"

-Rob Beint, Sous Chef, Meadow Gardens Golf Club

"You have an infectious spirit and nothing can dim that shine. I love that you are putting this on paper, sometimes we achieve greater things when we are faced with obstacles, finding our true meaning in this life. Your meaning is to interact with people and just by being yourself, you give them something they didn't have before. Thank you, Ryan."

-Ramona Laffer, RN

"One of your gifts is serving others. It's no surprise that you always find the optimism and through your experience and resilience, the ability to affect others and inspire them to keep moving forward. You have this wonderful talent of telling a story and leaving an impact with your message."

-Tanya Harrison, Friend

"Ryan you're an inspiration! Thanks for sharing, you have no idea when you're going to meet someone and have such an impact on them, and your life."

-Marc Campbell, Paul Dickson's Neighbour (look above)

FOREWORD

Ryan's role modeling of resilience is exemplified in his occupation as Chief Taekwon-Do Instructor in our community.

I continue to be astonished by his professionalism, modesty and lifelong focus on personal development. Quite honestly, my husband and I have been blown away by his instruction techniques. He teaches the students life lessons focusing on respect, modesty, self-inhibition, and emphasis on practice and learning. His teachings are short, clear, respectful and demonstrated actively, which helps non-auditory learning styles. He manages an incredible variety of students (ages, skill levels, self-regulation abilities, emotional challenges). The students know that he is in control but will always be patient and respectful. He has incredible patience with students who struggle with focus, attention and impulse control. They may not understand or value it at the time, but recognizing these qualities in such a dignified way is not a skill many teachers or parents are able to maintain.

Above all, he treats the students with incredible respect day in and day out, despite whatever they "bring" to class. They look up to him in so many ways and not the least of them is this quality. They may not all recognize it right now, but they are learning how to treat others based on how he successfully manages his class.

Dr. Melissa Paquette, FRCPC
Pediatrician, Royal Inland Hospital,
Clinical Assistant Professor, UBC

INTRODUCTION

Have you learned to laugh at yourself yet? I hope you have. Life deals out some pretty amazing stuff sometimes and if you don't learn to laugh at it, well this is going to be a rough ride for you! Why would you want to make it harder than it is? It's your choice. I'm sure you've heard it said, "Life is 1% what happens to you and 99% how you react to it". Obstacles will come your way, that's for sure; some you'll conquer, some you won't, and some will just humble you. I have learned to savour all three. The conquering ones are easy to enjoy, you win, you are victorious, and you get a prize - it is that simple. Some obstacles you won't "win" at, you'll learn to cope with or manage, which means you now know how to handle that obstacle, so you still win. Then there are those obstacles that will humble you and make you feel like you've got no chance - like thinking you could pee on the sun and put it out, or blow air out of your mouth and actually move the clouds. I just laugh when these things happen. I've been told that if you can laugh at yourself, you will always have material - and boy does life give you material! And if you are too arrogant to relax your sphincter a little bit and recognize these moments, life will be very frustrating for you. You've got to learn to laugh it off. Comedian Matt Rife explains it this way, "If you can learn to laugh at those things that should make you miserable, then that's how you win life!"

I know, some of you will debate this and won't think it's that easy. Perhaps you are right. Maybe it takes practice, like a learned skill. You weren't good at walking the first time you tried, I guarantee you, but you eventually got there. Coping mechanisms are learned responses and that skill can be developed. Next time you are angry, frustrated, or infuriated try saying the word "bubbles". I DARE you not to feel at least a little light-hearted! You have to be open to finding the humour in things. It's everywhere. Look at the duckbill platypus and tell me God wasn't laughing His butt off when He created it. Watch the "pedestrian crossing" light stay on just long enough for you to get in front of the first lane of traffic before it gives you the "hand" to stop. Try washing/waxing your car and watch it rain outside afterward. That is some funny stuff and I'm only just scratching the surface!

What about something like Parkinson's? Am I saying that it's funny to be diagnosed with a debilitating condition that has no known cause or cure? Maybe. I thought it was hilarious that I was diagnosed at the age of 43 - a guy who took his vitamins, didn't do drugs, didn't abuse alcohol, I exercised regularly and had my 4th degree black belt, was actively instructing, in otherwise great physical condition and had a happy loving home life with a beautiful wife and 2 fantastic kids. I was endlessly grateful for everything I had and had accomplished. I did all the right things to lead a healthy happy life: set goals, associated with a positive and uplifting crowd, etc. On any given day, I would say, "If I died tomorrow, it's been a good run and I have no regrets." I thought I would just grow old and slide into my casket without any maladies other than my time was up. And then I get Parkinson's out of the deal??! That's just hilarious to me!!! At its very core it's ironic, which is a basic comedic device. Maybe it's just me, but I'm gambling (quite "literally", with this book - is that a triple entendre?) that there are more like me out there. More people out there that seek to find the humour in things, not out of a disrespect for someone's misfortune, but hopefully to offer some levity in an all too serious world. None of us are getting out of this thing alive, so we might as well enjoy the ride. Hopefully, some of these

3

stories will bring a smile to your soul and brighten your outlook, especially for the newly diagnosed. I want you to know that it's going to be okay. It may not be the way you had once pictured, but who told you that you were in control? Potentially funny shit is going to happen all around you, and if you keep your eyes open, you'll benefit from it and hopefully learn to laugh at yourself, which of course means you've always got material. So buckle up, unclench your sphincter and enjoy some lessons and stories.

-Ryan

PS I don't have it in my heart to be hurtful towards you or anyone else, for that matter. If something I say in these following pages could be taken 2 ways and one of them offends you, I probably meant the other one.

MY STORY
(THE READER'S DIGEST VERSION)

I always wondered why knowing about the author should mean anything to the reader. It seemed like something I could skip, right? Not really relevant to the story? Then you watch one day of world news and realize how much perspective counts. It's quite difficult to see things correctly if you don't look at them from the right perspective.

I was born in a small northern British Columbian town in Canada. Geographically, it is in the middle of the province, but since the northern half is 99% bush, it is called northern BC. If you asked me if I had a normal upbringing I would say yes, but then again, what have I got to compare it to? Well, what other upbringings have you had as a frame of comparison? I will say one thing that seemed weird though, I always got along with my parents. All of my friends seemed to have problems dealing with the authority figures in their lives, but my older brother and I understood that when they were correcting our behavior, we had it coming! When we

5

had struggles, they were there for us, and when we did well they celebrated with us. We just got along. I remember one family dinner when I was home from university I jokingly suggested that my parents were either secret agents or aliens living out a longitudinal study on human behaviour by just acting like *normal* people because we got along so well. Sure we argued, but never out of hate or anger, instead for the sake of learning each other's point of view, more like respectful debates. My wife, who at the time was my new girlfriend came from a family where open communication was not as common and upon her first exposure to our "family discussions", she thought we were truly angry with each other! She wasn't used to this impassioned way of expressing your viewpoint and I would have to console her and tell her we were just discussing something.

I think I had a pretty normal functional upbringing and to the date of my writing this, Mom and Dad still live in the house we grew up in, with the same phone number and have been committed to each other for 50+ years. Love those two!

After graduating high school and serving as class president, I pursued the fields of psychology and physical education at university, and it was there that I met Sue. We met each other at a Taekwon-Do school nearby. I was teaching there when she came to train from another dojang

(Korean training hall). I remember that I was teaching a kid's class at the time when she walked in. "WOW! Who is that??" I thought. The kids started laughing at something. When I asked what was so funny, they informed me that I had just miscounted in Korean. It was lust at first sight, (love always comes after, I believe) she was B-E-A-uitiful as Truman would say. She looked like a young Meg Ryan but with silky smooth light brown hair, sparkly blue eyes, the most gorgeously adorable face I had ever seen AND she knew how to kick?? Oh wow! Later that week, we found ourselves both being third wheels at a party and hit it off - the rest was history. Our relationship began and six years later we were married and in ten we had our first child, Landon. Two and a half years later we got our second, Tana. These two have brought me more joy than I ever dreamed possible. We expected the best, and we got the best. Some say you shouldn't get your hopes up, which I've never understood because every good thing starts with hope and a dream. I say, "Get them up!" We were taught to be specific in setting our goals. We did and we got exactly what we wanted, gender order, age gap, and even hair/eye colour. If you've ever doubted that God answers prayer, how do you explain that?

We moved our young family to a ski and golf resort on the western skirt of the Monashee mountains called Sun Peaks.

It was there that we made our roots, the kids got their education in a fun, active, positive and safe community. When living at a resort you are generally surrounded by positive people. Imagine the dynamics of it: either they're on vacation (good mood) or they live there by choice, which means they are generally content. Have you ever been around people that aren't happy with where they are?? You want to remind them that they are not trees - "MOVE! Go somewhere you want to be!" Generally, if a person is unhappy, so are those around them.

School for the kids was on the ski hill, so either it was a hike each morning to school, or they took the ski lift during the ski season. Oh, and school was Monday to Thursday, Fridays were always off. Since the parental community designed and built the school, we chose the schedule. Living at a distance from groceries, physicians, dentists, etc. a trip to town takes a lot of the day. Or you could get an extra day of skiing in as a family. The standing rule at our school: on a snow day if there was 15cm or more snowfall overnight, Phys.ed class was first, then schoolwork! I teach my kids you've got to have priorities in life and enjoying the journey is definitely one of them. You can read more about this in my other book Always Push the Swing, a legacy gift for my children explaining how they were raised and what lessons I hope that they take into adulthood. It's a shameless plug, but hey, this is my book.

While living at Sun Peaks I continued teaching Taekwon-Do classes and was lucky enough to be woven into many students' lives and trained a lot of black belts, my wife and children being among them. I also worked for the flagship hotel in the resort which gave me many benefits such as access to the only pool, sun deck and 24 hour gym in the resort at the time, in addition to the usual extended medical/dental/insurance benefits of an employee. So in addition to the regular activity of skiing, biking, hiking, golfing, etc. I also hit the gym for workouts 3-5 times per week after my evening shift was over. Why after work? Well you are already sweaty and gross from work, nobody is crazy enough to be in the hotel gym at midnight, and my family was asleep so I wouldn't be cutting away family time for personal gains. Plus I could shower and shave at work and arrive home feeling fresh. One of my secret goals was to one day be like Ariel's father from The Little Mermaid, chronologically old, but physically youthful and strong. I wanted to be strong enough to protect MY little mermaid (and her mother and brother) from any harm that may come their way. Call it a male ego, or whatever you like - I like to be able to protect my family if I had to. This has always been important to me and physical fitness, along with good mental health, was the foundation for this. Mike Tyson was asked why he exercised at night? "Because my competition is asleep". I respected that. Why did I go to the gym after work? Because the average guy didn't. The average guy was sitting at the bar losing his money, his liver and usually his marriage. I never desired to be average. Average to me was the cream of the crap, the best of the worst, the worst of the best. Nobody strives to be average and nobody likes luke-warm.

Now, I was no Greek God or Olympic athlete, don't let me mislead you. I wasn't obsessively chiseled; I was just active and fit. Sometimes I would ski for the day, teach a couple Taekwon-Do classes, do an evening shift (8000-12000 steps), do a plyometrics workout at the gym after, and then ski home. Endless energy but when my head hit the pillow, it was lights out! People would ask, "Where do you find the motivation to do it all?" I would reply, "Motivation??" I would say, "you're thinking about it too much. You just do it." Many of my ex-co-workers to this day will say they remember when everyone else went out for drinks, Ryan went to the gym instead. I never was much of a "bar stool champion" but I never looked down on those that wanted to have a drink among friends. I just didn't want their results. Was I social? Oh, very much so, but my health, family and future were a priority.

One of my childhood heroes was Superman because A) he could fly and B) he was pretty much invincible. I was delighted to learn one day in my early adulthood that even my surname, Oevermann, was linked to Nietzsche's construct of the Übermensch, which loosely translated, meant Superman. I remember when some people's goal was to just feel human again - I jokingly didn't want to suffer the downgrade! I know, I know, that was inside my head though. I avoided being externally arrogant at all costs.

Then my early 40s hit and I started to wonder why my right leg wasn't keeping up with my left leg. My heel strike was getting clumpy in my gait vs. smooth and rolling heel-to-toe as it should. This didn't bother me too much and I tried some physiotherapy and osteopathy to try and resolve it. It's amazing what you can get used to. Soon I was experiencing a lack of mobility in my shoulder and hand dexterity was sometimes mitigated. Things like putting on a seatbelt or doing push-ups were becoming more and more tedious. Then I started to notice a muscle spasm in my leg occurring more often. It was more like a shake you get when your muscles are exhausted from trying to squeeze out that last push-up. It was a shake, but I could stop it if I focused on relaxing it.

In the winter of 2017, my sluggish right leg had made my foot strike the ground at the wrong angle so many times that it developed a stress fracture in my metatarsals. I wore a boot cast for 5 months trying to get it to recover. All of these issues by themselves were not major and I just wrote them off as being individual problems to solve. I had never been that old before so I didn't know how things were supposed to be - and you don't either! I also have a grasp on how intricately woven our body's systems are and how causality can be difficult to narrow down.

Sue had been doing a lot of reading and studying of medical journals. She was growing concerned, so we tried a few things to naturally address symptoms from adding MCT Oil to the diet, eating Ketogenically, increasing water intake, and even supplementing with CBD and THC (yup, good ol' Marijuana). We leaned down and felt better digestively, but my symptoms continued. Bradykinesia (as I now know it to be called) was making my handwriting and finger manipulation incredibly muted.

Then a visit to my physiotherapist, whom I often drove 2 hours to see and I respectfully called "The Body Whisperer", started to connect some dots. Something I had said in my appointment made him curious and he asked for permission to contact my family doctor, to which I whole-heartedly agreed. My doctor, in turn, made a referral to the Movement Disorder Specialist at the University of British Columbia in Vancouver.

On April 1, 2019, my wife and I were sitting in the waiting room at the UBC office. When we sat down with the neurologist, she explained that she had been observing me in the waiting room and in short order she was able to confirm my wife's and physiotherapist's suspicions - Early Onset Parkinson's. The neurologist was confident as this was her area of expertise.

I was gutted, as you might be with any such news. My first thought: Was it hereditary? Was it going to affect my kids? And then, will I become a burden to my family? I actually remember thinking why couldn't it be something terminal? At least that way my wife and family would be taken care of by my life insurance - way better than being a cost and a burden to them. It's one of the reasons I don't think that anxiety and depression are symptoms of the disorder per se, but a *result of knowing* something may be wrong yet not knowing what it is - it's a correlation at best, in my opinion. It's like saying that sleeping is a symptom of alcoholism. It isn't, you just happen to pass out after a big binge.

Later that day we went to my friend's place to stay the night. Bruce is, to this day, one of my closest friends and has seen me through a lot, always supportive, and never judgmental. He and his beautiful wife Tere were the first people with whom we shared my diagnosis. I remember sitting on their patio with their new fire table, still emotionally raw from the news that afternoon and I suddenly became optimistic. "Hey, if there was a medication for each symptom, then each symptom could be managed and it would be like I didn't have it", I explained to my wife. I told her, "We're all going to age, I'm just going to do it a little faster, that's all". I wasn't trying to convince anybody; this was the way I saw it, and still do in many ways.

So I took this news home and played it close to the chest for over 2 years. I told my parents and my brother what the neurologist suspected. I still wasn't 100% convinced but was willing to try the levocarb prescription to see if it would help. I just wanted to stop shaking mostly. Gosh, was that irritating! I could tolerate the lack of movement and a little pain can be managed, but this feeling of the whole world around me shaking or like you were riding on a ferry boat with that big vibration going all through your body, well that was enough to drive a person mad. Sadly, I responded well to the medication. As you may know, Parkinson's has no litmus test to confirm diagnosis. The physician notices a pattern, prescribes Levocarb, and if you respond to it, congratulations, you have Parkinson's.

Months went by and we were able to, through trial and error, find the right regimen of Levocarb and agonists for me. For anyone who noticed something was wrong, I simply told them that I was just low on dopamine and was trying a supplement to counteract it. I relied on the fact that Parkinson's was not well-known enough back then. Nobody ever put it together and that's how I wanted it. I didn't want the news out until I had told my kids - and boy did I not want to tell them! I'm grateful that Sue was with me upon diagnosis - who knows how long it would have taken me to divulge this news?! And now how was I supposed to tell my little babies that their hero, the guy that hung the moon, the guy that in their minds could/would do just about anything, had a busted brain and likely wasn't going to get any better? It devastated me, the thought of taking the wind out of their young sails like that. Up to that point, I believed that I could do anything if I put my heart and mind to it and now I felt like Superman when he became mortal. Remember, when he is in the diner and gets his ass handed to him after relinquishing his powers? I wasn't ashamed or embarrassed. I had done nothing, to my knowledge, to cause Parkinson's. I just didn't want my kids to face this negativity. It haunted me, but so did keeping it secret. It's what they call cognitive dissonance, and it can be very stressful, living a lie. I read up on things to say, how to say it to them, and what children need to know about PD, etc. but it petrified me. I DID NOT WANT TO DO IT, did I mention that part? I DID NOT WANT TO TELL THEM.

Now, my kids knew something was up, they weren't naive, but they were kids, busy with their own lives. At 14 and 17 they didn't have any major life concerns and I didn't want them to. They knew I was supplementing trying to fix something with my muscles, but nothing scary. I was active enough that I had nursed many injuries before and they were familiar with that. Heck, I took a ski to the face once and skied to the bottom backward and bent over so the blood wouldn't stain my new KJUS jacket! I wasn't invincible but my attitude was always resilient and unwavering. Well, I was almost ready to tell them in the fall of 2020 but my son was planning to attend film school the following February for 5 months, away from home. This leaving the nest was nerve-racking for all of us since he was only 16 then and he was going to be a day's drive away from home in a town he didn't know, living with a family he had never met. This was anxious enough, but he was just slightly more excited than he was scared to do it so I was proud of him. I didn't want to give him any reason not to take the opportunity. No decent parent ever wants to be the reason their kids don't pursue their dreams. So I kept it quiet until he returned in the summer.

On the summer evening of July 20, 2021 I sat my kids down. All 4 of us were home and I was as brave as I was going to get. Let me tell you it was one of the most difficult things I've ever had to do in my life and I promise you it was tear-filled. (I get choked up just writing about it now.) They took it well. I reminded them that people don't die *from* Parkinson's, they die *with* Parkinson's. It took some time for it to settle in on their minds but, as they are lovely human beings, they were nothing but supportive and positive. I may have got a few extra hugs and cuddles out of the deal.

Now that my kids knew, I didn't care if anyone else knew. In fact, the more the better. You see, some of my symptoms were becoming very noticeable. Sometimes I would slur my words because my mouth muscles wouldn't articulate properly. Sometimes I would stumble. What if one of my student's parents thought I had been drinking while teaching their kids? What if work suspected this and I lost my job? I was tired of living a secret. I have always been a very transparent person, I don't harbour secrets and I'm open and honest with people so this news getting out was such a relief! The community support and outpouring of love from friends and relatives was overwhelming, to say the least. I received messages of praise and support that one might only receive at a eulogy but I was alive to experience it. It was very, very humbling. Even the local newspaper did a 2-page story: "Local resident opens up about living with Parkinson's Disease" (you can Google it). I encouraged people not to take my "masked" facial expression or muted reactions as a personal slight, to not avoid me and think I wanted to be left alone. I loved social interaction just as much as I always had and didn't want others to feel less appreciated because of my limiting condition.

As of writing this book I am managing, although every day seems a little different and the waves of on/off vary. I try to time my phases with my full-time work and teaching, most of the time successfully. I recently hosted the first return-to-sport Taekwon-Do tournament since CoVid and tested successfully for my 5th-degree black belt. Anything I can do to tell Parkinson's where to stick it, I do it. I've been called an "undying optimist" many times and I continue to hold that view. I have my moments as we all do, but I can't be beaten mentally. I won't be beaten mentally.

Now it's just a matter of time for PD to figure that out.

Parky (PAHR-KEE) - abbreviated pronoun for someone with Parkinson's; neither diminutive nor derogatory; however, best used in first person as some people are just a bunch of babies.

Also, not to be confused with a similar sounding term, parkour (PAHR-KOR); similar letters but very, very different.

THE PARKY SHUFFLE

With Parkinson's you may display a variety of symptoms such as arm/leg tremors, bradykinesia (slowness of the muscles), tense muscles making you look very stiff, dyskinesia making you look like you're doing the "peepee dance" (a side effect of too much Levocarb), and festinating steps (short stride, quick step). I call this last one "The Parky Shuffle" and it drives me. Up. The. Wall. It's as if your muscles feel so weak that your legs are too tired to make a full stride, but you want to keep your pace so the feet speed up. It amazes me. One minute I will be walking full stride and then like someone hit me in the hips with a Botox dart my hips will no longer make a full stride but my lower legs want to soldier on in that "Eye of the Tiger" spirit. In my case, from years of Taekwon-Do training and lots of jumping involved, my calves are about the same size as my quads. I've always loved to jump - off things,

19

over things, on things - anything to get me in the air. Again, like Superman. Because of this gastrocnemius anomaly that I have developed over the years, at the time of writing this book I can jump over a five-foot obstacle and span a ten-foot gap from a standstill. When the "Parky Shuffle" kicks in, this sudden deficit of power to the hips is compensated by my calves taking over and I end up looking like I'm in a race with my knees tied together. I look like an elderly man who just soiled himself and is frantically trying to get to the bathroom before it shows. You know those first few steps you make when you walk into a store during winter and you scuff your feet on the carpet to get the snow off? It's like that but it continues throughout the store, you look like a god-damned Tauntaun from Star Wars. This comes and goes throughout my waves of medication and as I said it's incredibly frustrating.

Now I'm fully aware that some people have a pet peeve of scuffing feet. Long before I had developed Parkinson's I heard it said to others, "Hey, pick up your feet!". This wasn't directed at me, it was at someone else, but I became aware of this idiosyncrasy long ago. It used to be one of my wife's pet peeves, although I think out of love and compassion for my condition it has made her less judgmental.

I remember being in a store casually shopping and I was

in full "Parky Shuffle" mode as I would call it. A woman was standing within earshot of me and reflexively whipped a perturbed glare at the culprits - my feet. She didn't say anything, perhaps out of politeness (we were in Canada, after all), but I could nonetheless feel her disdain for my incessant scuffing. I understood, from her perspective, here is a physically fit, young-looking man, scuffing of the feet is just a sign of laziness! But she said nothing, verbally. Now even though her demeanor was politely maintained, her natural head-whipping reaction was loud and clear. I caught her eye and responded with a smile. "It drives my wife crazy," I said. She gave a slow, hesitant, confirming nod as if to say, "Go on..." This partially revealed her immediate and instinctual judgment but at the same time she withheld her criticism. I said, "You know who it really drives crazy?" She shook her head. "Me," I said with a disarming chuckle, letting her know that I was aware of what she was thinking but wasn't offended by it - in fact, I was on her side with it. My awareness and apparent frustration with it now known by both of us, it was clear to her that it wasn't by my choice and my light-hearted comment popped the bubble of tension she was withholding and her face instantly changed from rancor to empathy. We engaged in a friendly, understanding conversation about Parkinson's. I believe people at their core are genuinely nice but get misunderstood in the daily routine of life. Then I carried on with my shuffling, I mean shopping.

At the date of writing this, I still get frustrated by the shuffle-step. I'm learning to cope with it, but I have my moments. Many times, in my off phase, the dopiness is so strong that I have to trick my brain and count the tiles on the floor to get anywhere. I don't claim to have the answers to all of the frustrations that PD patients go through. I'm going through this for the first time, perhaps like you. I've often said, "I'm as old as I've ever been!" meaning we're all going through life, learning, and each of us is at a different stage, and we don't always know the solution to the quandaries that life sets before us.

In the meantime, I've set my ringtone on my phone to LMFAO's Party Rock Anthem in which the line goes "Every day I'm shufflin'". Hey, if you can't beat 'em, join 'em!

SOMETIMES YOU WIN, SOMETIMES YOU LEARN*

One time I was about to leave the grocery store and another lady appearing in her early 60's was entering my path heading for the door. With a hindered stride I've learned to be more aware as I never want to be that guy that's in front of you and holding up traffic. Plus the shuffle step is embarrassing and you can feel it when you are a spectacle, which makes the condition worse, like a form of muscular anxiety, self-perpetuated by the knowledge of being watched. (I've never before realized how loud the silence can be when a disability is displayed. The silence, by the way, is the onlooker's way of portraying their inability to modulate their reaction). Out of a gentlemanly habit and clear knowledge of my own temporary limitation, I insisted the lady go first because she would be faster, to which she replied, "I don't know about that!" I then noticed that she too had limited movement. We ended up "walking" towards the door together and I said with

23

a smile "I'll race you then?" She laughed. We got outside and I asked what has got her hobbled. I like to address the elephant in the room and I've learned if your heart is in the right place, it's never offensive. She told me it was ALS (amyotrophic lateral sclerosis, aka Lou Gehrig's Disease) and she was just diagnosed 3 months ago around Christmas. My heart sank. I know that you don't die from Parkinson's, you die with it, and I'm aware of many cases where full healthy lives are lived despite the condition. ALS is far more invasive, like Parkinson's on steroids. When it shows up, it comes with a deadline. The muscles deteriorate over a remaining life expectancy of 2-5 years. She asked about my condition, shocked by my youth, and we had a brief and slightly emotional conversation. With her permission, I gave her a gentle hug and we parted ways wishing each other the best. Later I was frustrated with myself, wishing I could have been more encouraging for her at the time but one of the things that is also hindered during this "off state" is the ability to relax and speak clearly (again, like a muscular anxiety). The dopiness during this wave of Parkinson's affects articulation of words and your ability, therefore your desire, to speak is limited. When you're not good at something, even temporarily, you tend not to do it, it's that simple. I vowed to make a greater effort the next time I come across an opportunity to connect and encourage someone who has been plagued with such discouraging news - at least get their name for heaven's sake, Ryan! I had to let go of the disappointment in myself and hope that the hug I gave her was enough. Sometimes you win, sometimes you learn.

MOVIE TIME!

My kids and I share the love of movies, something they definitely got from me, not my wife. Not that I'm a deranged fanatic by any means, but God bless her, her naivety of pop culture and entertainment is shocking. So I took it upon myself to educate our kids on the classics. We would have space exploration education nights (Star Wars), sports history lessons (Rocky), crime and punishment sessions (Shawshank Redemption and Green Mile), stress management courses (Dumb and Dumber) and animal exploration classes (Ace Ventura). In addition to raising well-rounded, intelligent, compassionate human beings, I also wanted them to be relatable. My daughter grew a specific love of Marvel movies. Classics? Debatable, but definitely impactful on society and so, relatable. Can't say I didn't share the same love.

We finally got to go and see the newest Marvel movie, I think it was Guardians of the Galaxy at the time. It was a Daddy/Daughter date, one of many that I will cherish forever and one day fondly look back on. We sat down in our seats, popcorn at the ready. "Daddy, why didn't we get the nice seats?" my daughter asked. The movie theatre had 2 rows of D-Box seats that had interactive motion and a subwoofer that shook the chair during action sequences. It was an added effect to make the feature presentation more real and enjoyable. Truthfully I had wanted to sit there, but when I selected the seats at the box office, there weren't 2 seats available together. Coming out of CoVid this was typical; nobody wanted to sit right next to a stranger and so seating availability was spread out because sitting 6 feet apart from each other prevented you from sharing the same air, right?? Right.

Being the loving dad that I am but with a sense of humour, I explained to my daughter that they only had one seat available and I would have felt guilty sitting in that one and enjoying the movie by myself in full D-Box effect while she was back in the cheap seats. So being the gentleman that I was I opted to sit with her, in the regular non-vibrating seats. By now my kids know my sarcastic tone and have even learned a thing or two about appropriate retorts and timing. She calmly replied smiling, "Why would you need one, Daddy, your seat shakes anyway?"

That's my girl - guts and timing!

STUPID LEG

Public bathrooms are not my favourite thing (and the crowd gasps). The smell, the uncleanliness, the degenerate disregard for a clean seat or flushed toilet, the crass bodily functions that some let loose amongst the anonymity of enclosed stalls - and that's just the ladies' bathrooms I have accidentally gone into. Recently the stiffness in my body and limited strength in my shoulder have made some basic movements difficult. At the risk of being too indelicate, the simple task of wiping had become a tedious task. The obvious civilized solution at home was to install a bidet. Now, in North America, bidets are not that common and really only appear in high-end, regal hotels. Most North Americans "poohpooh" the idea of washing their backside instead of using their beloved "TP" and think a small geyser up the tailpipe is gross and unsanitary. I vehemently disagree, in fact, I would maintain that it's the other way around. Not only is it a cleaner way to complete your business, but the archaic act of wiping is ineffective and uncivilized. Flat out, wipers are gross! Yeah, I said it. Don't believe me? Walk with me down "Rational Thought Lane" for a second. Imagine you're meandering along the beach and a seagull christens your head with its defecatious blessing from above. Would you just reach for some paper towel, scrub your hair with it, grinding the excrement into your scalp, and then say, "There, that's good enough" and carry on with your day feeling clean?? Heck no you wouldn't! You wouldn't feel clean until you what? Got your head under a sink, a tap, a shower and at the very least, rinsed your head thoroughly. Et voila, the bidet! By the way, what would you think of that individual who was just satisfied with scrubbing it with a bit of paper towel? Gross, unsanitary, nasty, primitive, I could go on. In one of the cleanest and most civilized countries in the world, Japan, bidets are quite common (according to NPR 80% as of 2016) and highly developed with all sorts of pampering options (warm water, front/back spray, air dry, sounds for discreteness, deodorizer, etc.). The Japanese culture are renowned for their cleanliness and they think using toilet paper is of the caveman era. So, just so that you are aware, those of us who commonly use a bidet are wondering what the heck the rest of you monsters are still doing with toilet paper! However, I digress. The point is I'm not excited when I have to use a public bathroom. I now understand how the character Shitbreak felt in the classic comedy, American Pie.

Anyhow, while reluctantly using a public stall one day it occurred to me while sitting on the porcelain throne in the mall what it must sound and look like from the outside of a stall with a Parkinson's patient in it. You know how most bathroom stall walls only come part way down, not all the way to the floor, leaving your feet exposed either to your neighbour or the people outside of the stalls? A Parkinson's tremor is often felt in one of the legs, indicating a repetitive, shaking movement occurring. Some of you see where I'm going with this and I'm guessing most are the males. You see, when a guy is in a bathroom stall, by himself, and his leg is shaking, what might it look like is going on in there to an outsider? This haunts me to this day and I can tell you that each and every time I am in a public bathroom stall I am cognizant of what it looks like from the outside. It's borderline uncontrollable and so sometimes you just have to do what I do: finish your business, zip up and walk out looking exhausted and say to the onlookers, "Whew, that was a tough one!" You've got to roll with the punches, friends.

A SUPER SHOPPING EXPERIENCE

One of my weekly to-do's is the household grocery shopping, and I keep a pretty stocked fridge, freezer and pantry. Despite this, however, "there's nothing to eat" is one of the most common phrases uttered by my family. You too?? Crazy. It's amazing how I can create a full 10 days of meals on "there's nothing to eat". Must be a special gift handed down from my mother but not easily absorbed by my 1st world children. I know what they mean to say: "why is there nothing quick, easy, somewhat healthy and already made in front of me right now?" Nonetheless, I love having them around and will still cherish every minute of it while they are here. More on this in <u>Always Push the Swing</u>.

This one particular day, after running errands, I had an hour to do the shopping and then get to my Taekwon-Do classes on time. Kids/parents depend on me to be there and greet the students at the dojang as many of them arrive directly from school. So the countdown was on, adding a bit of anxiety I don't enjoy. You see, normally an hour is plenty of time to do shopping in one store, but bradykinesia and my Parky Shuffle are kicking in, which means relatively that store just got a whole lot bigger! Steven Wright, the famous one-liner comedian, says "Everywhere is walking distance if you've got the time." Well, I don't have the time, because if you cover ground at a fraction of the pace, this giant store just became the size of Disneyland. You try covering Disneyland in an hour!

I've made it to the entrance of the store, where I would normally just swiftly walk in with a cart shop away. Instead, I'm standing there, by myself, feet not wanting to move and trembling. (I'm guessing this is what they call "freezing".) What do I do? Do I return to my vehicle and forego the shopping, or do I continue on and begin my sojourn through the store for all to witness my newfound ineptitude? I've learned from many good mentors in my life to become a problem solver, not a whiner and so my brain, without ego, goes to work on a solution. I cut my losses, ate my pride and asked the customer service clerk if they had any motorized carts I could borrow. She said, "There's one left, here you go" and she handed me the key pointing at the corral where they are stored for charging. At this time I'm 46 years old and often accused of being in my early 30s, in good physical condition, a 4th degree black belt and I've been reduced to using a motorized cart that, in my mind, has been reserved for the obese and the handicapped. This was a tough pill to swallow, but it seemed the logical solution to my conundrum. I sucked in my tears, gritted my teeth in frustration and shuffled over to the cart. (By the way, if you ever want to simulate the shuffle-step, drop your pants around your ankles and try walking at your normal speed. You might consider wearing safety gear and a private location.)

Now, I have never been on a motorized shopping cart before, and I'm doubting the customer service clerk had been either. This *should* be straightforward, turn the key, and hit the throttle. So I unplugged the cart from its charging station and sat down on the seat. We live in a litigious society so there are a multitude of default warning messages on the steering column. In any other country it would have read "Good luck" on it or "Keep rubber side down", if that. Not in North America. Here we must put warning stickers that say things like, "Don't put hot drink in crotch" and "this is paint, don't eat it". These labels are necessary because we must cater to the lowest common denominator of intelligence, and courts support this. I tell you, when we start putting things like "do not perform brain surgery with this ski pole", we may be in

33

trouble as a society.

Anyhow, I turn the throttle. The electric beast groans alive and rolls forward with electronic swiftness! Okay, this could work, I'm off and running, here we go! The cart goes 30 metres and stops, dead. I need to mention here, it doesn't slow down, "run out of gas", it stops, like on a dime! I have no idea why. It is electric so it does not idle or coast and it has one gear so it's either moving or stopped. In this case stopped dead, in the opening intersection of the store. There are other customers around, but nobody is watching me closely enough to notice that there is a problem. If there was, I'm sure they would all be thinking the same thing: "there's just a handicapped person in the way, I'll give him his space and go around him the way a polite person would." I stand up, which must baffle any onlookers seeing a seemingly mobile individual using an electric shopping cart. I look for any hidden obstructions, like a log in front of a horse in tall grass. Why has this thing stopped?? Remember I'm still trying to choke back the tearful pride of having to use this thing in the first place, now I'm adding frustration to the mix. I try the throttle, no use. I turn the wheel, no use. I rock it to get it going, no use. I somehow discovered that if my feet were hovering at just the right position above the ground, beside the cart it would move. No idea why, but it seems to work.

For another 30 or so metres. Now I'm in the middle of the store. It's too far to walk to the exit, I'm too choked up to find words, and too infuriated and short on time to do anything about it. I'm not going to be that "crazy" guy that has a meltdown in public, trying to draw everyone to my problems. Equally so, I'm frustrated that NOBODY IS NOTICING THE HANDICAPPED GUY HAVING AN INTERNAL MELTDOWN IN THE MIDDLE OF THE STORE. Why would they though? They're not inside my head. I'm wearing sunglasses inside (it's the best way to hide tears), on an electric cart, in a city's big-box grocery store - who wants to have anything to do with that???

You may ask, why didn't you just ask for help? I know, you'd think it's that easy, right? Remember, my pride has been decimated being in this situation already, my eyes are full of angry tears, my throat is choked up and of course my voice is weakened and my speech is garbled. Communication is not one of my strengths at this moment. But resilience is. Some would call it stubbornness - same coin, different side.

I continue my frustrated dance with the motorized cart, trying to find just the right sequence of movements to make it work, like a cheat code on a video game. Chunk by chunk I get my shopping done and it takes nearly the full hour that I had. I wheel up to the checkout and the stupid thing stops

4 feet from the cash register. Have you ever just cut your losses and ditched an old dead car on the side of the highway? Just grabbed your shit and walked away from it, never to return to it again? This was me at this point. I told the lady behind the till, "That thing is more handicapped than I am." I loaded my things onto the conveyor belt, again choking back tears of frustration with the whole situation. As she rang up my items, I tried to keep pace with her. Oh, right, this by the way is one of the stores that has abandoned grocery bagging as a service which means you get to play "employee", organize and bag your items yourself, and also keep pace with the amount of time it takes the checker to go "beep" with a barcode. And, in the interest of environmental friendliness (which I fully endorse), you've got to use your own bags (if you've remembered them), but they don't give you a rack at the ergonomic height to hold the bag open like the clerks have and so you have to fumble at an awkward height to keep the bag and its handles open with your third hand while you pack your items in! Sound tricky? Yeah, and that's WITHOUT Parkinson's. Now add tremor, weakness, anger and frustration.

During this whole process, I realized, "Where am I going? I could barely walk on my own, let alone carry full grocery bags." I looked back at the electric cart staring me down, broken down and still abandoned in the entryway of the checkout. I suppose I could try and make it work again, just to get to my vehicle. I explain to the clerk in my weakened mumbled speech that this was all new for me. She was still in a bit of shock, not knowing how to handle the situation, making 2 of us, and inquires "Bad back?" I reply, "No, bad brain". "Oh," she says in a yeah-don't-want-to-touch-that-one kind of manner. I asked, "Can these carts go out to the parking lot?" wondering what the process is here and how they have this planned out for their handicapped shoppers. She asked a co-worker if the carts go to the parking lot and got a "no they can't leave the store" response. What??! Do they think Scottie BEAMS handicapped people to the entrance of the store?? How do they expect the groceries to get into the car? It must have been a combination of despair, confusion and WTF look on my face, but one of the service clerks nearby recognized it and said "I will help you". Thank God, what a relief! Anoush's name tag could've had a beam of light shining down from heaven and I couldn't have appreciated him more. After what seemed to be an episode of non-stop obstacles for the past hour, Anoush's "I will help you" was music to my ears. His simple act of compassion to carry my 3 or 4 shopping bags out to the handicapped parking stall (something I was also still getting used to) was

37

overwhelming. I gave him a heartfelt thank you and tried to offer him money in appreciation, but he refused. It was his pleasure to help and I didn't want to cheapen that; I know how he feels to be able to do something nice for someone. It's worth more than money, and to accept the money can devalue the act of kindness. Respect Anoush, respect.

I climbed into the truck I was driving. Again, the perceived contrast of a disabled person able to climb up into the driver's seat of a truck but not be able to walk 10 metres must have been confusing to anyone watching. This has reinforced the philosophy "don't judge" in my daily habits and has made me a more compassionate individual, looking for that individual in the store who needs help but is too proud to ask for it, that duck on the water that seems calm, but deep down the feet are scrambling. There's always help needed you just have to have an eye for it. I drove away, with the emotional blending of frustration, humility and gratitude, much like those old school sinks where the hot water tap and the cold water tap are separate and your hands combine the two feeling separately both hot and cold, but not warm. The tears dried up on my face before I got home. And I have since taken advantage of one of the greatest gifts that came out of CoVid - the curbside delivery. With a little advanced planning and usually for a couple bucks you place the order ahead of time, and someone else does the grocery shopping for you and brings it to your car. As for the social benefit I usually would get out of shopping, I balance it out with visits from good friends with the time that I save. Take that electric cart!

WHAT'S SHAKING?

Friendly greetings vary from culture to culture, and I can admit that in our North American English-speaking world we can be ethnocentric and always want to think ours is the correct one, but in reality, none of them make sense! Even my word processing program has English U.S. and English Canada as options.

Aussies, who seem to be quite abundant in a Canadian ski resort, would say "How ya goin' mate?" If you didn't know any better that would seem like a strange inquiry to a North American. It's like when you're young or nervous to speak and you try to say one of two common phrases like "How are you?" or "How's it going?" but instead, you muck it up and combine the two, feeling like a buffoon. "How you going?" is just a tongue-tied blunder. What do you mean "how am I going?" By foot! Silly wanka. To us it's like taking "good luck" and "take care" and instead saying "take luck". But alas, this is their friendly way of greeting you, and it's <u>always</u> good-natured. The "mate" part I still question as I learned that meant something TOTALLY different in science class growing up!

In the notorious & culturally entertaining province of Newfoundland, a common Newfinese greeting is "Whatta y'at?" - loosely translated this means "What are you doing?" The correct response, "This is it." Wow.

A Korean would greet you by saying "Annyeong haseyo", literally meaning "Are you at peace?"

Arabic greeting, "As-Salaam Alaykum" means "Peace be upon you". This sounds more like a farewell than anything.

So many different ways to greet people around the world, but if you get the gist of it, someone is wishing you well, in their own way. It's important not to get hung up on minutiae and take it for what it is - being kind to one another, something we could all do with more of these days.

So I go walking into one of the local restaurants one day and my boss, Steve, is sitting at the bar doing some work. It's mid-afternoon and the place is pretty empty, with only a few workers and a couple customers around. Now Steve's dad has Parkinson's, we've had many heart-to-heart conversations, Steve and I. He has been nothing but supportive and encouraging in my employment while living with PD.

He smiles welcomingly. "Hey, Ryan! What's shaking, my

man?" he amicably shouts out. Now at different stages of life, questions can have different impacts on you. This one now had a potentially different interpretation.

I laughingly replied, "Gosh, Steve, everything!" and smiled the best that I could.

The place fall apart with laughter. Steve's hand instantly slaps his forehead! "Ahhhhh, Ryan, I am so sorry!" he smiled sheepishly, "I didn't even think..."

"It's all good," I replied and we laughed together.

There are a variety of answers to this common question, so be sure to have one ready for when you get it. If it hasn't happened to you yet, it will. And of course, be willing to laugh yourself!

GETTING CARDED AT 47

"Do you have picture ID, sir?"

(Is this cracker kidding me?)

I'm not one for racial slurs, and a white guy calling another white guy a "cracker" seems a bit redundant at first. But this guy was white on white bread. If Caucasian had a poster child, he was it. Not only that, I remembered him from 20-odd years ago in the local nightclub scene where I did security work. He was always trying to appear "black". Much like famous comedian Tom Segura, many white people get enamoured with black culture and understandably so. If you are a young guy trying hard to fit in and you watch a lot of popular sports like NBA basketball, NFL football, or rap music videos, the chance of you being exposed to black culture is, let's just say higher than average. This guy would come into the club wearing a baggy basketball outfit, gold chains, crooked flat-brimmed PHAT hat or a brightly coloured velvet leisure suit and bright white kicks. He was

43

trying hard to be MTV cool, but his frumpy Gru-like build and sizable ears made him look more like a white Forest Whitaker. Amongst the black American culture, he would be called a "whigga" - a combination of the words "white" and you know damn well what the other word is. It's a term that has never been acceptable, except possibly amongst black people, and I'm Caucasian, I know my place - but don't you pretend to not know what the word is. The point is he was a unique and memorable individual, but he always seemed nice and never caused a problem. I remembered him.

"Do you have picture ID, sir?"

I was in a BC government liquor store buying some thank-you gifts for my custodians. They had been especially helpful to my Taekwon-Do school lately and a case of "man-flowers" goes a long way to show a little appreciation. Now, the liquor law in BC states that if you appear under the age of 40, you may be asked to produce proof of age in the form of government ID. If you appear under 25, 2 pieces of ID. I knew this since I had worked in the food and beverage industry for over 25 years, so naturally, I respected his request and took it as a compliment. Having lived through the CoVid years, I was used to producing proof of vaccination and picture ID, which many carried on their mobile device. I produced for him a digital version of my driver's license, complete with date of birth, picture, address, height, weight and eye colour.

"I need the actual ID, do you have it?"

"Yes, it's in my car."

"Would you go get it?"

(What in the...?)

"Sure."

I should point out that I am wearing golf shorts, a brightly coloured golf shirt TUCKED IN, and white Nike cross-trainers which I have come to know now as "Dad shoes" - none of which says that I am under the age of 40, let alone 19, the legal age required to purchase alcohol in BC. But, he was just doing his job, and I respected that, so I obliged him and went to the car.

Being in a Parkinsonian state, I shuffle-stepped off to my car where my 77-year-old mother was patiently waiting. She notices I'm empty-handed and says, "What's wrong?" I reply, "I'm being carded." She laughs, "You're kidding?! Pfffffff!!" I shuffle step back inside the store and back up to the till. I pull out my driver's license and present it to him. He analyzes it with a surprised look on his face as if he realized he made a huge misjudgment in age. He then says, "Do you have a second piece of ID?" (Wow. Ok. He's only doing his job, don't make a scene I think to myself.) I hand him my credit card with my name and signature on it. "Do you have one with a picture on it?" he asks. Now I know for a FACT that the second piece of ID only requires your name and signature, not a picture. I handed him my firearms license, another credit card, my bank debit card, my Costco card - any of which would be acceptable as a second piece of valid identification. "Okay," he says. By this time, I'm a little baffled and to be honest the frazzling has induced typical Parkinsonian tremor and dyskinesia. Again he's just doing his job but in a little too "be all you can be" sort of way. My wallet is now disemboweled onto the counter and I'm freezing up. I tried returning one of my cards to my wallet, having difficulty getting it to slide in - a typical PD occurrence. "Sorry", I stammer in true Canadian form, "I have Parkinson's and have trouble with dexterity. Would you be kind enough to help me get my cards back in my wallet?" He obliged, I paid for my beer and left with a mixture of feeling complimented by the age confusion and victimized by a clerk "just doing his job". Then I smiled and remembered that this guy for the rest of his days has to know that he carded a 47-year-old man with golf shorts, a tucked-in shirt, Dad shoes and Parkinson's - a disease characteristically exhibited by the elderly!

STARING IS CARING?

I cannot believe how many people stare! Grown adults even!! One of the first things you are taught as a child regarding social etiquette, at least in our part of the world, is that it is rude to stare. It does not matter why: large nose, missing appendages, extremely good looks, extremely bad looks, a pimple on someone's forehead, etc. Austin Powers exploits this when he sees a giant mole on Fred Savage's face in Goldmember. It's funny because everyone can see it, it's huge, and Austin fails miserably at being discrete about it. Whatever the "oddity" is that you observe, it's considered impolite to stare because whatever it is can't be helped. Even blind people have been known to "feel" when someone is staring at them. It's awkward, for even the most comfortable of souls and the most familiar of people. Try staring at your child or your spouse and don't say anything. How long does it take for them to get uncomfortable, wigged out, and tell you to stop.

Depending on your situation you may experience this in one way or another and you'll just have to come to terms with it. (The more subtle version of staring is the deafening silence or pause in conversation, just what you want when your feet scuff!) It may be easier for some than others. Some of you may really not care what others think. You'd proudly walk naked through a farmer's market without a care in the world and if that's you, congratulations, and happy shopping! You will have an easier time with the staring that may take place with Parkinson's.

While still confident yet humble I had to come to terms with this common social faux-pas and rationalize a way to not build anger or frustration towards others. This frustration would only create negative energy and that just robs you of enjoying life. I had to realize that the more somebody was disarmed and caught up in the stare, the more shocking it must be for them. Whatever behaviour you are exhibiting, whether it's bradykinesia, dyskinesia, belaboured speech, or the Parky Shuffle, it's the contrast between what is expected and what is being displayed that intensifies the shock and awe that the onlooker is experiencing. Did you catch that? Think about it, would you be taken aback by a golfer wearing wild coloured pants on a golf course? Not at all, that's weird in some settings but commonly expected on a golf course. Wear those same pants to a funeral and you're going to get some strange looks and comments. It's the contrast of what's expected vs. what is being observed.

In my case, at first glance, you would see a physically fit (but not muscle-bound), mid-30s-looking male who dresses well, is personable and friendly, relatively well educated and seemingly capable of managing quite well in society. Take it a step further, if you see my Taekwon-Do school decal on my car or the "Instructor" on my jacket, this would take you further away from a "handicapped" image. And then you see me walk like a Tauntaun trying to wipe the shit off his feet and you'll hear a proverbial record scratch. What? Why? How? This doesn't compute. All of these things are going through the onlooker's mind and they are left disarmed. Disarmed of the social safeguards they have been taught of keeping your mouth closed and not staring. It's intriguing, and they are trying to reconcile what they see in their brain. The point is, it's a compliment! It means you don't otherwise appear disabled or handicapped and so this behaviour is shocking for the onlooker. Should they look away?

Social etiquette would say yes, but they are unable to. Their social conventions are disabled and they are temporarily paralyzed. Who's handicapped now??

LIFE HAPPENS

We've all heard the phrase "shit happens", right? Something goes wrong and you want to lighten the abysmal mood with a prophetically deep and apathetic thought and you come up with the overwhelmingly creative "shit happens"? I've always found this phrase to be a pessimistic dismissal of all the good things that can/do happen to us in life. My dad always taught me that there is more good in the world than bad, you just have to have the right eye for detecting it. Even as kids, when we would have a complaint about something he would hear us out and then ask us to list 2 positive things about it, whatever "it" was. With this type of upbringing, you get good at seeing things from an optimist's perspective. I was taught in my early adulthood to expect the best, speak what you want not what you don't want. Speak positive into life as if your words were seeds that fall to the ground and grow. When you learn to train your mind and your tongue for success, watch what happens! You will start sounding different, you will start living different, and you will start feeling different. As you do this however, you will begin to notice how poor everyone else is at this skill and it will challenge you. "Do I step out and sound different and be 'Mr. Positive' or shall I not upset the herd and keep doing the same. Just listen, it's easy to pick out why most people are floundering or failing at their goals. My friend calls it "diarrhea of the mouth". Absolute garbage comes out of most people's mouths and you'd think they were TRYING to sink their own ships all the time!

Basic psychology will tell you that your mind essentially works in visual form (even for the visually impaired). If I say the word "horse" you most likely, without even trying to consciously conjuring the image, picture a muscular four-legged hoofed animal, even if only for a nanosecond. We also know that we gravitate towards what we focus on. Try riding a bike in a straight line while looking to the side - you will eventually veer towards that side, and most likely crash. I confirmed this just last month biking with the kids and trying to take a video of them riding beside me. The road rash has almost healed up, but it will still leave a mark. This is applicable throughout life, if you focus on a goal, good or bad, obsessively you will inevitably move towards that goal in some way, shape or form. Thus the phrase, 'keep your eyes on the prize'. Now you may ask, "why would I focus on a 'bad goal'?" This leads us to the next key part of the equation.

Our subconscious mind has difficulty managing negatives. What do I mean by that? If you say, "I'm not going to get sick" your mind ultimately has to picture your perception of "sick". Images of laying in bed, feverish, stuffy eyes, etc. So basically you've just HIGHLIGHTED to your brain to focus (and manifest) "sick". Inadvertently you are programming your brain to focus on being sick! You might even try and trick your brain and use the present, like affirmations do, "I am not sick". Tell me, what does "not sick" look like?? Now, what does healthy look like? I'll be willing to bet you can more easily conjure pictures of healthy than "not sick". Some of you may be thinking I'm splitting hairs here, but I'm not. We know these things to work! Norman Vincent Peale, Gary Smalley, Ben Sweetland, they've all been writing about this for decades. Just because you may not be aware of it doesn't make it less accurate.

How about this one, don't think about a stop sign. What did you just picture?! With that in mind, think about all of the things that people say that sink their own ships. "I can't remember," "I'm so broke," "I don't want to be fat" and "I'm getting sick." All well-intended and maybe honest things to say, but if you have a mindset of success you realize why most people are their own worst enemies. Each one of these phrases inspires your brain to conjure the image of exactly what you're trying to avoid, and as we gravitate towards that on which we focus our lives can end up being in shambles and we wonder why. Isn't that amazing?!! Congratulations, there's your crash course in Basics of Success 101 - get your words together! Call it Hung By the Tongue, you get what you speak, As A Man Thinketh, etc. and you might think it's a bunch of hooey but there's a whole section in your local bookstore dedicated to this topic, written by people who have proven these concepts time and time again so it must rank of some importance.

Here's a quick little example you can try, that will support this. Next time you see someone and you're sure that you've known their name in the past but it's not coming to you right then, try reprogramming your reaction. Most likely your learned response is to shake your head and say "I forget", "I can't remember" or the killer, "I have such a bad memory". That destroys all initiative your subconscious has in even trying to recall. Picture a little worker in your brain who is always on shift and working for you. They manage the "files" or long term storage so-to-speak of your brain. You see a person walking towards you and the little worker instantly goes to work frantically digging through files looking to find the name that is definitely somewhere in your database, and you say "I can't remember?!" You just arrested any efforts the little worker in your brain is going to employ by basically saying "you suck at your job, there's no point in trying, just stop." Without emotion or hesitation, the little worker closes up the filing cabinet and moves on to the next job. Well, why wouldn't that be the reaction? I mean, you just told the worker that it can't be done and you're the master in charge! Well is it YOUR brain or isn't it? They aren't giving out second-hand ones much these days; you're likely the only owner, so take charge of it. Next time try this, when you see the person you recognize and your brain starts scrambling for the name you're having trouble with, say (even if only to yourself) "I know their name, it will come to me." Immediately that little worker searches even faster, now encouraged by its master, you, and within seconds the name will "DING" and come down the chute and you will "remember" it. Try it, I double-dog dare you! Will it work every time? Maybe not, but a heck of a lot more times than with Mr. I. Forget and little Ms. I. Can't!

I tell you all of that to explain to you why I use the phrase "life happens" instead of "shit happens". A pessimistic viewpoint is just life-draining. If you've really given up you may justify and call it "realistic" or "pragmatic" as if a fancier word justifies the energy leak in your life. Ever hear of a "turd in a tuxedo"? Optimism inspires hope and energizes you to do more, be more and enjoy more. Shit happens, but so do good things. Life clearly isn't all bad, and if you want to avoid some unnecessary shit, then stop talking unnecessary shit. Accept the good that could come into your life and be open to some positives. It'll happen more times than you think, and if nothing else you'll be more grateful, which is a whole other topic inspiring good mental health. Michael J. Fox once said, "If you don't think you have anything to be grateful for, keep looking. Because you don't just receive optimism. You can't wait for things to be great and then be grateful for that. You've got to behave in a way that promotes that." Great wisdom.

Many years after I have written this book scientists may have identified a cure, the cause of Parkinson's or at least some correlations with it. I don't know what I have or haven't done to develop PD. It's just one of those things, "life happens". I didn't spend much time, post-diagnosis, trying to figure out why this had happened. It already happened! Modern medicine, at the time, didn't have a clue what caused PD, so why would I be so arrogant to assume I could figure out why or how it came to be?? Sure, being a patient of a mysterious condition I accept that I'm a piece of the puzzle, but I'm no physician, so I didn't expend much mental energy on figuring out how or why I had developed Parkinson's. When teaching self-defence to students, whether men, women or children, it's a very small section determining why your attacker attacked you, and it's usually done after the fact. The attack has already commenced, so what are you going to do about it? That's where I was at, mentally, just after being diagnosed; what am I going to do about it? I have, as I write this, just achieved my 5th degree black belt in Taekwon-Do, having previously medaled nationally in both pattern and sparring, and taught students of all ages, sizes, and skill levels. I promise you, if you throw a kick to my face I will spend very little time trying to figure out why you did it. I'm already reacting to it and hopefully landing my response to it before your foot makes contact. After the incident is settled and I have you under control I may have some questions for you but not during the assault. I spend no time crying over spilled milk, I just move.

Now I don't want to minimize the shock, discouragement and disappointment my wife and I went through in hearing the news that I had Parkinson's. "Early Onset," they said, as if it sounded better. It was the same deal I was just younger than the typical age range for PD. Tears were shed, let me tell you, but even before that diagnosis day was up I remember telling my beautiful wife that "there was hope. If they have a medication to help with each symptom, then it'll be like I don't have it." I'm not sure who I was trying to cheer up, me or her, but life happens.

NOT ALL ROSY

Just so you don't think I'm a Pollyanna and everything is all sunshine and unicorn farts there are some times that you will go through that will challenge your resolve. I have been there more times than anyone will every know.

One night, while I was working as a waiter, I was delivering food to a table and my Parky shuffle was in full effect. It had been vexing me off and on over the past while and it was beginning to take its toll on me. Just the concept of walking along full-stride and then suddenly there's an invisible lasso around my knees was aggravating enough. Try driving your car at highway speed and slamming it into first gear and see how your car handles it. Frustrating wouldn't sum it up, especially if you're on the clock. Anyhow, here I am at work shuffling as best as I can to a table and there's a lone lady at the bar working on her second glass of wine. Now, I'm aware of the response that my shuffle step evokes in onlookers. Usually, it's a quick notice of the feet, an immediate shift of focus to the face and then normally a poker-faced neutral expression as if nothing is up or the quick recovery, a darting glance away. These are the socially polite responses. On occasion, there's an empathetic "Are you alright?" expression or inquiry which, although this might reveal a person's innocent naivety or just politeness, is a caring response and certainly welcomed. I would always rather address the elephant in the room with a caring person than it go undiscussed. THIS cold-hearted barstool champion took one glance at my feet, one wide-eyed look at my face and laughed out loud. Not a small chuckle, or an accidental guffaw covered by apologetic restraint - a full-on laugh in my face as if to say "HAHAHA LOOK AT YOU, YOU PATHETIC CREATURE!" I'm always one for a laugh, I love comedy in all forms, and I am quick to laugh with someone, sometimes to a fault realizing afterward it might be the wrong time to laugh. I assure you I did not laugh. I didn't even twitch while making eye contact with her. My face returned to her a confirming response that there was nothing comical occurring, that I was not performing some party trick for her benefit. She kept laughing as I continued to the table. I have to admit, it was a weak moment for me mentally. It hurt, nobody likes to be laughed at, especially when it's something they can do nothing about. My first thought was not a mature one and it did indeed involve the ladies eyeballs and a rusty spoon. And then logic kicked in: what kind of a cold-hearted douchebag laughs at a handicapped person, because of their disability, to their face? The answer: a very sad, pathetic one; an individual that is small in character, lacking in human decency and devoid of basic human respect. I instantly felt a great sense of sorrow for her and carried on about my work. Not so much sorrow that I wanted to stop to befriend her and maybe remove her ignorance by having a nice conversation. No no, let's not be confused here! She was human garbage in my opinion. You might ask, did I say anything? No, I didn't. Do I regret it? No, I don't. What could I have said that would make it better? You see, I'm not like her, I don't feel better by putting someone else down. I believe the only time you should be looking down on a person is to help them up or to help tie their shoe. "Putting her in her place" would've fallen on deaf ears, potentially put my job in jeopardy, definitely caused me stress and affected my work. And what would it have accomplished? I learned a long time ago to not waste words with idiots because they will bring you down to their level of idiocrity and beat you with their experience. So no, nothing was said, and unfortunately, there was nobody within earshot to otherwise speak up in my defense.

And yes I just coined the term idiocrity, it's like mediocrity but specifically for idiots.

I am however ready for that one condescending and judgmental person in the parking lot snapping "You don't look very handicapped," to which I will smile and reply, "And you don't look very smart either but I'll give you the benefit of the doubt!"

IRONY

Irony and sarcasm, partners in crime these two are. Irony is when something happens which is the opposite of what is expected. Sarcasm is a verbal form of irony in which the speaker communicates the opposite of what is. I'm well versed in sarcasm, and when asked if I'm being sarcastic I usually reply with a deadpanned "No, not at all" or "Moi??? Don't be silly". Only a select few can detect it and those who catch on are my people. I believe the English call it cheeky, but it's always fun-intended. It's often accompanied by a dry sense of humour and those that practice sarcasm regularly would view it as a higher form of intelligence, which is debatable. A quick search of memes on the internet can give you a feeling for the perspective from which a sarcastic person views the world. Here are a few examples:

"Sarcasm (noun) - the brain's natural defense against the less intelligent."

"My level of sarcasm depends on your level of stupidity."

"Sarcasm (noun) - the tactful ability to insult idiots without them realizing it."

These are rampant, and not altogether positive, so I try to avoid using sarcasm, but sometimes admittedly hard to refuse from a comedic perspective.

Irony is slightly different and a little misunderstood. As mentioned previously, it's when something happens that is the opposite of what is expected. Many would think of Alanis Morrisette's song "Ironic" where she lists off a slough of examples of what she thinks is ironic. Unfortunately, they are not actually ironic, merely coincidental. "It's a free ride when you've already paid" and "a traffic jam when you're already late" are not ironic, they are just unfortunate situations, and are not typically what one would define as ironic. It IS however ironic that she wrote the song from a position of authority on the subject, but "failed", all the way to the bank. The song, despite exhibiting incorrect examples of irony, earned her a Juno Award and a Grammy Award nomination.

Keeping the theme of being able to laugh at yourself, irony is also a form of humor. I have, for most of my adulthood enjoyed a primarily healthy life by doing all the right things. I don't consume alcohol much if at all. I don't consume or experiment with narcotics or recreational drugs. I take a healthy regimen of organically harvested vitamins daily. I don't smoke and still can't figure out why anyone starts. I have lived an active lifestyle by way of regular gym workouts, skiing, hiking, tennis, Taekwon-Do, and generally partaking in any activity offered or enjoyed by my social environment. I have purposefully avoided typical rut-system lifestyle stresses evident in most middle-aged males. I have chosen healthy places to reside in, void of environmental pollutants and toxins. I have pursued mentally healthy endeavours always trying to better myself in one way or another. I have even employed a skincare habit to retain my youthful joie de vivre. With all of that in place, I get Parkinson's??! HA! That's irony at its finest! I did indeed laugh, if only on the inside, at the preposterousness of this result from that recipe of healthy living. It's laughable for sure, but definitely ironic.

READ THE SIGNS

I'm not entirely sure where life is going, but I recognize that there is a time to be in the driver's seat and create your life and there's a time to follow the signs and see where you're destined to go. The trick is to know when to do each one. At this point, I feel like I am to follow some signs.

This is Brian. Brian and his wife came into my workplace this past spring visiting from Australia, a common occurrence at this time of year in a Canadian mountain resort. When Brian walked slowly through the door with his cane, being led by his loving wife, I was able to pick it up right away. Brian was a badass in his day, a day when if you got a tattoo you had earned it, like a badge of honour. You didn't just have an inspirational Zen moment and a $100 of white privilege to burn (well, how many tattoos do you see on non-whites, hmmmm?). He appeared to have stories to tell from trail time well served. He had clearly earned the love and devotion of his lady (whom I later found out to be his wife of 54 years, Barb). They were on vacation and visiting for one night as many of the tour buses do. Brian's demeanor appeared to be plagued by more than just aging, however. I now know how my neurologist felt watching me those years ago in her clinic waiting room. Mitigated movements, slight tremor in the hand, weakened step - Brian had Parkinson's.

I greeted the couple at their table, once the host had settled them in, "Good evening, my name is Ryan, I'll be looking after you." They both returned a smile and the traditional friendly Aussie "How ya going?", Brian's smile was muted by his condition, again I could relate. I asked about their day, as I do all of my guests. We shared some polite banter and then I inquired by pointing at Brian's cane, "What's got you hobbled?" Addressing the elephant in the room, I find, is easy when your intentions are genuine. Barb replied, "he has Parkinson's". I reached out my hand and said

"I thought we had something in common." Now, finding out this news is never met with a resounding joyful response of welcoming brotherhood, but rather a freezing of the moment and a sincere connection of eye-locked empathy. Brian reached out and we shook hands - pun intended. As engaged in our conversation as they were, they were equally confused, which I have also become used to. I look too young to be plagued by such a condition and my abilities while my medication is working are relatively good enough to hide the beast's symptoms, at first glance. I assured them they would notice soon enough as my walking gait and speech would become hindered as the waves of Levocarb would metabolize and fade away.

Since I related to Brian's condition I was able to cater to their needs better than I usually could, which after 27 years as a professional waiter can be difficult to step up. Serving is a tactful combination of etiquette, psychology, and people skills, an art form that when combined with genuinely good intentions has yielded me and my family a pretty good living. I take pride in my work, no status required, I'm literally serving my "fellow man" like the good book says to do. Some people think it's sales; I would debate that sales is just service, filling a person's needs and being rewarded for it. I was able

67

to do the seemingly little things for Brian like asking the chef to cut his steak because of his probable weakened dexterity in the hands, bring him a spoon because eating salad with a fork can drive a Parky fucking crazy, and just give him time to speak when I know all of his thoughts happen at normal speed but the articulating speech muscles won't keep up. Heartfelt empathetic notions of "I understand and I see you", are something we all crave as humans.

We shared stories throughout the experience with brief interactions. Brian was a Vietnam vet and used to box regularly. In addition to his regimen of common Parkinson's meds, he had been recently trying medical Botox treatments to curb an overactive muscle contraction in his shoulder. His wife shared that he had his low moments on occasion, which is also common in Parkys - although I maintain that this isn't a symptom but a response to knowing you have PD. I shared that I had been training Taekwon-Do for many years and had just returned from competition with my family and we had been successful on the podium. "Anything I could do to give Parkinson's the proverbial middle finger," I explained. Brian chuckled as the fighter inside him related to this.

While I was away from the table, I later found out, Brian had welled up in tears as he was inspired by my optimism and active living despite Parkinson's. Barb informed me of my influence when I returned and she explained that Brian had decided to take up boxing again. Her eyes were glossy too as it had been a while since her husband had a glimmer of hope in his eyes. He was inspired to re-engage in his fight for his life as he knew it to be. What a humbling and wonderful result of our brief interaction and connection! I had to take a moment myself in the back as the quickening emotion of the moment overcame me; the unique and yet impactful impression I could make on someone so different from me and yet so strongly connected by this crippling condition.

I don't like my condition. However, I'm an undying optimist and I adjust my sails to harness whatever life blows at me. PD is not something I would have anticipated or chosen, but I do wonder now if it's not a stepping stone to greater success. It was unbelievably rewarding to be the source of encouragement for a gentleman easily 30 years my senior, and who had been in a drought of hope and ambition in life.

Once again, fuck you Parkinson's but also maybe thank you Parkinson's? The adventure continues...

THE GRATITUDE HABIT

I'm not sure if this is a journal entry, a message that belongs in my other book to my children <u>Always Push the Swing</u>, or if it belongs in this book, but here it goes.

I don't know where in your health journey this message finds you, but I'm here to remind you, that no matter the situation, there are good days ahead. The future is still bright if you have the right attitude, but you are going to have to learn the ability to harness the energy of what lies ahead. To borrow from the world of sailing, you will have to learn to "adjust your sails". You see, the wind is going to blow, that's a fact. I always say, "life happens. What are you going to do with it?" The mere concept of sailing requires harnessing this energy and productively redirecting it. I understand that sometimes adjustments are necessary for this to happen, but it is possible.

The late business magnate and Amway co-founder Rich De Vos gave a wonderful talk on the 4 Winds - North, South,

East and West.

The North Wind is an icy cold wind that can send you running for cover. I am paraphrasing here of course, but there's not much you can do about this one except ride it out. In the world of Parkinson's this would be accepting the waves of medication and using your time effectively. When you are on, you are on, use it! It's valuable time. I am writing this in what some would call the middle of the night. Why, because right now I am on and my brain/body is working, I can see clearly, type effectively, etc. Does that suck? Would I rather be sleeping? Honestly, I'm not sure as I learned long ago from Rich's talk to use the North Wind to my advantage and have gotten so accustomed to it that I don't begrudge it anyhow.

The South Wind is usually a light wind. A sailboat can't really use light wind to propel and as a result can be called "dead in the water". A boat that is dead in the water is out of control. So how do you handle this? In the words of Dory from Finding Nemo, "Just keep swimming, just keep swimming." If you found yourself in a boat, without the power of wind, what would you do? Paddle! Ask for help! Anything, but goddammit move! Don't sit there.

The East Wind has unsettling conditions, don't let them scare you. Don't let them steal your ambitions just because the conditions aren't perfect. Parkinson's hasn't blocked your road in life. It may now be part of your life though and you may have to make some changes. Okay. What, this was not in your plans? I know, but whoever told you that YOU were in control? It's a myth, an illusion, adjust your sails and move on. Rich says here, "The conditions are never right, they are merely something you deal with."

The West Wind is a good steady reliable breeze. This wind is more of a test to see how you handled the other winds. Are you in the right position and what have you done to deserve such a wind? Be careful, though, this can be where you can get a bit lazy, take your proverbial feet out of the pedals and that apathy could result in calamity.

Have you noticed anything about these winds? First, I would like to point out the ratio of good to bad winds here. Some would say it's 3 bad ones to 1 good one. Well, those people missed the point. It is 3 opportunities to prove your grit, perseverance, or steadfastness and one to so-call harvest the benefits of that work. There is an economy of this, on which I will expand later in this book. Second, none of these winds are created or stopped by you, they just ARE. That means their occurrence is out of your control, only your reaction to them is in your control. You may want to read that line again before moving on.

Borrowing from the world of aviation, you may be

surprised to learn that such things as "altitude" and "attitude" are directly related. The angle of the craft (attitude) uses with the force behind it (you staying positive and persevering) against resistance (stuff happening to you, obstacles in life, Parkinson's) to raise the craft (you) to a new altitude (better life). Wow, you may want to read that line a few times before moving on!! Please note, the craft must be moving forward AND resistance is NECESSARY for lift to occur.

In the world of martial arts, a relatively non-percussive art of Aikido teaches you to use your enemy's energy against them (or for you) by redirecting it. Either way, it's not just being defensive, but using the "bad" for good! Taekwon-Do is a defensive martial art also, but if my block smashes your shin bone you're less likely to kick at me again. I call it "offensive defense".

I offer the opportunity every few months for my Taekwon-Do students to test for their next belt level. I just finished examining 26 of them last night and now I have 4 hours of video footage to carefully review in the grading process. You see my handwriting cannot keep up with what my brain sees as they are performing their moves so I video it and review it later when I can write coherently. This is a direct and positive change that Parkinson's has had on my life. The good news is the camera catches everything and I

73

can review their performances in detail and offer good critiquing and coaching afterward. The bad news is the camera catches everything and I can review their performances in detail and offer good critiquing and coaching afterward.

Before I sat down to begin grading, I took the opportunity of being awake earlier than usual to take our puppy for a scooter ride. She's a 10-month-old cockapoo and she fits perfectly in a shoulder-sling bag that I can wear while scootering around my small village in the mountains. We stopped by to see my wife on her coffee break, to see my son as he arrived at his work, went for a morning cafe mocha in the morning sun and attempted the daily crossword puzzle. I bought the e-scooter as an environmental and economical choice for commuting to work and back in a fun way; since my walking ability has been unpredictable at best it's a nice coincidence to have it. Having said that, I did enjoy a nice walk with my kids and puppy last night after the belt examinations which was a real treat to be able to do.

Now I'm back at home, the puppy is exhausted from our adventures and napping in her bed, and I am here with a grateful and appreciative heart. I am 5 years into my PD diagnosis, having trouble walking, tremors, balance depleting, sleep inconsistency, anxiety-inducing DBS surgery on the horizon and who knows what other health issues are on the rise either related or unrelated to Parkinson's (remember I didn't see this one coming) and yet, I'm loving life! I am grateful for my kids, my wife, my friends, my community, the love and support that I've received. Gratitude is a habit you create and it energizes you. I believe it can defy science by surpassing the impossible perpetual machine because the energy you derive and share from your decision to be grateful multiplies and far outweighs the initial investment. Energy multiplied by gratitude, it's a habit you can create, and share with others, like I'm doing here now:)

Now I had better get to work on those belt gradings...

USE YOUR WORDS

Have you ever had a revelation or realization that a word or phrase didn't mean what you thought it meant? We've all had that experience haven't we? Please say yes so I feel better about what I'm about to tell you. You know, a discovery from looking at things from another perspective?

I'll give you an example. The phrase "I appreciate you", we understand to mean "thank you" and it's said in a heartfelt, grateful way. However, if you dissect the wording, it can actually seem a very arrogant thing to say. The word "depreciate" we all know means to lessen in value, correct? Well then, in turn, the word "appreciate" means to raise in value - much like ascend and descend are opposites. So the phrase "I appreciate you" means "I raise you in value", as if to say, "I am the subject here and with me you're worth more." See the potential arrogance?

I'll give you another one. When you're feeling sick, one might say that you are nauseous. Really? How rude! You see the word nauseous describes "something that causes a feeling of nausea or disgust", like being toxic. Are you saying I make you sick? I am the thing that is disgusting??! The correct word is nauseated, and people mix this up all the time. If you are feeling ill, you feel nauseated. By what? By something that is nauseous. Saying that someone is nauseous is just mean, like saying they are disgusting. It's our language and it often gets changed out of accepted ignorance.

Last one, then I'll tell you what I did. Do you know the phrase "rule of thumb"? Commonly used in our culture, isn't it? A driving instructor might say, "In this case the rule of thumb is...." You might casually tout that "As a rule of thumb I would..." What's this rule then? Well, if you look at the source of the phrase, it dates back to an archaic time when IT WAS LEGAL TO BEAT YOUR WIFE WITH A STICK NO WIDER THAN YOUR THUMB. Yeah, that's the rule of thumb! At a time in our society when people are identifying with different pronouns (which I'm not against but I can't relate to), in a time when using the R-word for a person with a mental deficiency is notably frowned upon (personally I'd like to bring this one back, my brain is by the very definition r-worded and I admit it), at a time when spanking your child is considered by some to be abusive, we're still running around morally preaching about our rule of thumb?!! Don't even get me started on "Indian summer"! Oy vay.

Now, I HIGHLY encourage you to Google some terminology with regards to Parkinson's. Educate yourself. I know, it's not fun, I didn't want to either! Heck, I didn't for quite some time! It can be daunting to read about symptoms you might experience, especially when you aren't experiencing them yet, and no one is to say you ever will! Do you know anybody that Googles their symptoms and scares the daylights out of themselves on the regular by their potential "online diagnoses"? I have family that do this and it drives me crazy (another word you aren't supposed to use, or so I am told). Anyhow, learn some basic terms so that you can better communicate with your caregiver or neurologist. Me, I, this one right here, was reporting to my neurologist about the "dyskinesia" I was experiencing from the Levocarb. Over the course of a few years, we tried different dosages, frequencies, times of day, and experimented with different agonists, dermal patches and pills. Then one day, my lovely wife came to an appointment with me and noticed the neurologist demonstrate dyskinesia and she turned to me and said, "That's not what you do. What you do seems to better fit the description of dystonia." Well, shit. She was right. And I'm pretty sure my neurologist wanted to transfer my file at this point. I had been reporting the wrong symptom! This would be like telling your physician you suspect you might have cervical cancer because you have been experiencing intense pain in your neck. (The cervical section of the spine in your neck is a fair distance from your cervix, if you have one and you would know if you did, to which words cervical cancer refer.) Easy to confuse, very, very different method of treatment.

So adjustments had to be made, of course, with this revelation of knowledge that I was experiencing dystonia vs dyskinesia.

In my defense:

- dyskinesia is the involuntary movement of a body part or the entire body that you can't control.

- dystonia is the involuntary stiffening or contraction of a muscle.

Doesn't that essentially sound like the same thing to you? Both are contracting muscles (the thing that makes muscles move) and both are unintentional. Both are common symptoms of Parkinson's and can be related to long-term use of levodopa. You can see how I confused the two, and you might too. Until you watch it, and HO LEE SHIT are they different. It's like saying a canoe and an aircraft carrier are the same thing because they are both vessels that float on water. Learn your symptoms so that you can communicate properly. To sum up, use your words.

RIDING SHOTGUN

It's an old term, and it's still used to this day. Maybe you've said it when jumping into someone's car. It means riding beside the driver, in the front seat; but this job also bears great responsibility. In the Wild West era of US history, a "shotgun guard" used to ride alongside a stagecoach driver as his protection, keeping a keen eye out for bandits and highwaymen. When we call "shotgun" to secure the front seat, it's a reference to a once-vital job. Now the role is a little less risky, depending on where you live of course! Today the shotgunner's responsibilities are to keep the driver awake and focused on the road, to help navigate, the organizing of snacks and drinks, music and control other passengers' behaviors - anything that may otherwise distract, deter or enable the driver's role of getting everyone to their destinations safely.

Much like the "shotgun" position, you may find yourself being a supporter of someone, in this case, who has PD. For those that aren't experiencing Parkinson's firsthand, don't think you aren't part of the equation! I have a groundswell of compassion, empathy, and appreciation for my wife as she is my life partner and thus this affects her too. I was more sad to realize that my wife had to watch me battle and ultimately deteriorate than I was to be diagnosed. It can't be easy to watch your best friend fumble, stumble and exhibit the ever-so-frustratingly feeble behavior that Parkinson's puts you through. Heck my friend Corey was genuinely angry that I had been dealt this card in life, not at me but about his friend being "ripped off". There is a whole slough of emotions you may go through while facing such a challenge as Parkinson's, whether you are the patient or the caregiver. The support that is received from those around you, even if it's just patience and understanding, is enough to make a strong man humble.

I've never wanted to be one of those people that cause issues, that is always a nag or an inconvenience in someone's day. I don't edit my order at a restaurant; if there are 1-2 things in the dish I don't care for I order something else or I just suck it up like a big boy. When I go grocery shopping in a store I am very consciously aware of my surroundings so that I won't be in your way - I have always been this way and I just find that common decency. I don't even like being in front of you in traffic, for crying out loud! Parkinson's is a tricky bitch, however, and it will change the way you look at some activities and even the simplest of actions. You will see life in a new light and with that I thought I would offer some insight on how you can make life a little easier for your loved one who has PD.

First off, the shock of feebleness can be hard to take. A Parky will at times be challenged by limited and weakened movement and I guarantee you this will lead to frustration for even the most enlightened of Buddhist monks. Give them the grace to falter and be frustrated, and learn to come to peace with it. You can offer help, knowing that you might get varying responses. Some people have pride to overcome in receiving help and may resent having to accept it - remember that it is not you that they are frustrated with. Some may just appreciate your assistance. Hopefully, it's the latter, but be prepared to forgive them. It's difficult to face these challenges and please understand that normal social graces may be hindered. Even though I am a strong proponent of the phrase "there's always time for manners", even a simple "thank you" could be mitigated or muted by hypophonia (soft speech, especially resulting from a lack of coordination in the vocal musculature).

*Side story: In my younger adult years, I did nightclub security, for about 10 years to make some extra cash. My background in martial arts and people skills lent to an ability to conflict-manage both verbally and physically, if necessary. At a night club, people come out to have a good time, be social, maybe dance and usually get a little loose with the help of "liquid courage". I have always enjoyed watching people have a good time. Likewise I have always loathed when others sought to rob someone of said good time. In one of my other books Always Push the Swing I reference a philosophy that I taught my kids: "It's always ok to have fun as long as it's not at the expense of someone else's". Well, in the night clubs when alcohol is in the mix (and who knows what else) this would happen occasionally throughout the night. I don't know what it is about North Americans, when we drink, we seem to think we are Mike Tyson and want to fight everyone (especially whisky). Nonetheless, if there was a scuffle or maybe you were just too intoxicated, you became a liability to the business and its patrons and you needed to be removed from the premises. In the province of BC, in a liquor-serving establishment, if you become deemed "undesirable" by the staff you may be asked to leave. Not leaving is considered an assault called "assault by trespass", and in this case, you can be justifiably removed from the premises. So basically if you didn't remove yourself, someone on the team was more than willing to help you with it - that's where we came in. Now I have never been a violent person, but swift justice I would happily serve, without prejudice. Whether you had been aggressive with the waitress or were just a little stumbly-bumbly, we were going to "help" you to the exit. If I was there to remove you I can honestly say that to this day, every person I physically ejected from the premises (and it's easily in the 1000s), whether I walked them out gently or had to open the door with their forehead while in an arm-bar, deep in my heart I said to myself "they are probably a good person when they are sober, forgive them for they know not what they are doing." I'm sure I read that somewhere growing up, but this was my mentality, not to judge a person by their worst moments. Even if they continued to challenge me once outside. Many times that same person would return one of the following night or weekend with their handshake out (which I was always cautious of) wanting to apologize for their behaviour the night previous. They would say something to the effect of "I was a real jerk, and it sounds like you could have done a lot worse by me but you didn't. I just wanted to say I respect that and I'm sorry. Thanks for not kicking my ass." The point is if I can forgive an intoxicated stranger, I think you can handle a little quip from your frustrated Parkinson-afflicted spouse. Empathy goes a long way. End of side story.

I've mentioned before about my festinating steps, and I've often explained Parkinson's as a form of muscular anxiety. This anxiety gets worse when people are watching. I have faced the humiliation of having to walk across a room with my shuffle steps and the silence by everyone around is deafening. People try to be polite and not say anything, but in actual fact, the silence is worse! The whole room quiets down just to hear your scuffing feet. For those of you, like me, who can't tolerate the sound of mastication (chewing food), well this irritating behaviour is now being caused by you, there's almost nothing you can do about it, and everyone is paying attention - trust me when I say this is 100 times worse. What's the best way to handle this? Continue what you were doing, or conversing about. Don't make a spectacle out of the Parky, they're embarrassed/angry/frustrated enough as it is. Like a good friend in the bathroom, give them some "cover fire", make some noise and let them carry on with dignity.

A big one for safety is to keep the area tidy around your Parky. Clutter on the floor, congested hallways and stairwells, are difficult for the patient to maneuver around, especially if balance is affected. Edges of carpets, shoes scattered in the coatroom (ahem), and ridges in the floor, all pose hazards. Remember, in an "off" phase, what seems amazingly simple to you is a tremendous task for the patient. They may be placing all of their focus on just operating the muscles to balance and make a stride, and dodging simple obstacles may be too much.

Where do you walk in relation to the Parkinson's patient? As a husband, I was taught to be a gentleman when walking with your bride into a building or event and that is to walk in front to keep your loved one protected against any forthcoming danger UNLESS there is an usher or guide, in which case the lady goes in front of you. (It isn't always ladies first.) I know it's old school but I find it is still classy to treat a lady as a lady, with love and respect, by being a gentleman (thanks Dave Duncan). With Parkinson's, there may be times when the patient is using every bit of concentration just to make steps and if you enter their pathway or walk across in front of them it causes distress and may cause them to stop or even fall. Since most of us don't remember our first steps as a child, think, if you will, when you first learned to ski on snow, or water, or any new sport. You were shaky, uneasy, unstable and every ounce of your brain was working on keeping you vertical. It's much the same for the Parky. If you can give them a wide berth and stay out of the area they are walking towards it will be hugely appreciated. I have personally found that if you enter my pathway, even 20 feet in advance, I will be forced to alter my step or even pause and let you pass because the management abilities to maneuver are being too taxed. Imagine walking through a crowd!

Here's the rub: walking behind them, or politely "letting them go first" isn't a great idea either. Remember that anxiety one feels when their feeble condition is on display? And remember many of us don't want to be in the way or inhibit other's moving, so walking behind a PD patient is also not desirable.

I'll be the first to admit, these aren't easy challenges to deal with and the solutions aren't so simple. However, if your Parky is a loved one, do what my loving wife does. She walks beside me, holding my hand, going at the pace that I can go. With that kind of love and compassion, you can change the world. I love my wife for so many reasons, and this is indeed one of them.

What about the basics of personal care? With mitigated muscular control and dexterity some basic dignities can be troublesome. Dental care, get an electric toothbrush. That simple rhythmic oscillating movement of brushing your teeth can be tedious and you don't want to neglect your oral health. There are many brands of decent powered toothbrushes on the market, most of which are recommended over a manual toothbrush anyhow, so go shopping. Buttons or fasteners on clothing can be cumbersome. You may wish to opt for snaps on shirts, slip-on shoes, etc. Wiping, as I mentioned previously, can be an arduous task - get a bidet. They are relatively inexpensive, attach easily to existing toilet seats (and are far more civilized in my opinion).

Many times a Parky's behaviour or movements (dyskinetic or bradykinetic) can appear strange to an onlooker. We realize this - we're neuromuscularly challenged, not idiots. And I can laugh with the best of them, make jokes about my condition and make light of situations. I remember Michael J. Fox when he fell over saying "hello" to a female passerby. She felt terrible but hadn't done anything wrong. He sprung up and laughed it off saying "Wow you really knocked me off my feet!" That's good stuff! My kids saying "Daddy, your theatre seat shakes already" or my friends joking that my wife no longer needed a vibrator because my shaking hand didn't require batteries, all of that I can handle. What hurts for me personally is someone mimicking my behaviour. It sounds obvious at first, but have you ever responded to your mumbling friend by mumbling back at them? Or walked strangely like imitating the George Jefferson walk for comedic purposes. Mimicking a Parky's movements is hurtful, even out of innocent jest, because currently it can't be helped, and they are most likely infuriated by it already. I've asked my family to make all the jokes they want, I can take it, but mimicry for me cuts deep.

Packaging. OMG packaging. Due to the prevalent dishonesty amongst the human population, merchandise has become so packaged up that it's easier to get into Fort Knoxx than it is to get your God-damned printer ink cartridge out of its package. I'm here to tell you that even trying to open a produce bag at the grocery store may now be a challenge for a Parky. Hand dexterity may be decreased, muscular strength limited, blurry vision from medication side effects - this is all a very frustrating situation. With this in mind, the next time you go to wrap a birthday or Christmas gift for your PD friend or family member, leave the duct tape and cable ties alone. (yes I have given gifts like this in the past:) Maybe go with a gift bag and decorative tissue paper instead of wrapping and taping. Again that every-eye-on-you moment of opening a gift can be stressful.

A big concern for me, especially when I hadn't told anyone yet about my diagnosis, was the way I would make others feel as a result of my lack of facial animation and expression due to a symptom called masking. Masking is the lack of motor function in the facial muscles causing the face to droop and look unimpressed or sad. Imagine a heavy wet cloth draped over your face while you are standing up. I have always been an excitable, energetic and outgoing individual so for me to not light up at somebody's compliment or jovially engage in comedic fashion with others with full undeniable joy on my face was odd and I didn't want another person to feel shorted, slighted, or not appreciated enough due to my lack of enthusiasm. It could be something as simple as waving while you drive by and I was too slow to wave back, or you cracking a really good joke and me laughing like Nien Nunb in Return of the Jedi while co-piloting the Millennium Falcon with Lando Calrissian. (By the way, for those of you who get that reference, first of all, congratulations, and second of all, that is a balls-on example of what it sounds and looks like.) What about telling your Parky spouse that you love them and not getting that twinkle-in-the-eye response back that you were once used to? It hurts, and we know it, and it hurts us more because our true delight is masked and you are the one that has to suffer from it - it's not a good feeling. So try not to judge too quickly or take our responses to heart. Give us some grace when it comes to any reaction that requires muscular motor movement.

Remember that Parkinson's can affect all neuromuscular ability, even in muscles like those used in retention. When a Parky has to go to the bathroom it may sneak up on them like a freight train going 1000 mph. In the past my body has put me on polite notice, saying "Hey, when you feel like it, and only if it's convenient and pleasing to the court, you might want to consider pulling the car over and looking for a nice bathroom". With Parkinson's, it's more like a large megaphone in your ear saying "YOU ARE GOING TO SHIT YOUR PANTS, NOW! MOVE IT SOLDIER!" So just be aware. All muscles can be affected.

While we are in the neighbourhood of delicate issues, sex. I am not sure in what stage of life this book finds you but I am still in my 40s, and I look forward to my 50s and 60s, etc. Sex drive remains, even with PD, very high but can be a bit more tedious now. Keep in mind muscles are affected and often weakened so you may have to make some adjustments, but if you are in a committed relationship remember to stay that way, committed. I joked earlier about my shaking hand being a sexual benefit to my wife, and yes this was a joke, it's not a benefit. Asking for sex in your relationship can become a challenge and anxiety-inducing, as this new condition runs deep and can affect the feelings of self-worth. Keep an open communication channel with your partner if they have

Parkinson's, and remember that they are still the same sexual being that they were before. At times you may have to take the initiative more than you have in the past to both remain sexually satisfied in your relationship.

Along the theme of Parkinson's rendering as a type of "muscular anxiety", those instances that normally just cause a little nervousness now become heightened and the ability to deal with them "Cool Hand Luke" style is diminished. (I know, I really dated myself on that one!) Any form of conflict-managing, public speaking, stress-inducing conversations, triggering events, or anything that might normally run just under the radar is now magnified 100X for the Parky. Even anticipation of these events I have found to limit and delay my "on" phase. Sometimes these situations are avoidable and sometimes not, so be prepared. I don't like being rushed or late for something, it causes anxiety normally, but with PD you can not cover up that anxiety - "you are made" as they say. No poker face can curb the revealing tremor that follows when this stress is felt. How do I handle it? I make sure I am early for appointments and I don't push it. This helps me remain calm and not shaky. Trying to rush a person with Parkinson's is like trying to do 250km/h in a Toyota Prius, something is going to go wrong. Try to understand this when your Parky wants to leave for an event before you normally would. They may be planning to have an "off" phase and there's little they can do about it except to prepare.

Bottom line, patience, compassion and forgiveness will be your best tools in helping you to be the best support for your Parkinson's-afflicted loved one. As I wrote to my friends in 2021 when announcing my diagnosis, "Continue to expect the best from me and forgive me when I fall short".

ACCEPTION AND HUMBLE PIE

First, we need to clarify what I mean here by "acception"; I am specific and quite particular in my choice of words. This word was once used in the English vernacular and has since become obsolete - well I am bringing it back! It is no secret, my propensity for clearly written communication, and with that, the proper employment of particular words. Many words in the English language get twisted and contorted over time and "evolve" into new meanings. That seems a bit careless to me if you plan to document history using words that can one day have a different meaning. Changing the meanings of words? Doesn't this defeat the purpose of communication over time? What if the word I am using today means something totally different 1000 years from now? When word meanings change, documented history can literally change - no wonder there are discrepancies and feuds about the validity of religious texts, territorial borders and the like! In my lifetime alone the proper meaning of the word "faggot" originally meant a log, then it meant a cigarette and now, well now you just don't use it if you have any respect. Words change meaning by their usage. My grandfather used to "burn a pile of fags in the field". Can you imagine if he said that today?! Dangerous this evolving of words. Before I get too far off topic, let me clarify my usage of the word "acception" so that some of you can relax your sphincters.

To "accept" something is a stative verb meaning to receive or come to realize. Except is a preposition meaning excluding. Thus an exception is something you exclude, and logically an acception is something you come to realize. These 2 words accept and except are often confused and used incorrectly: much like irregardless (there's no such word) and regardless, "I saw it" versus "I seen it" (the latter just wreaks of banjos and dirt driveways), or the all too often brutalized by the British "I was sat there" versus the correct phrasing "I was seated there" or "I sat there" (the UK has their own version of hillbilly too). If you are a social media user you may be quite familiar (and shocked) at how few people can properly employ the words to/too/two, their/there/they're, its/it's, your/you're or then/than correctly. If you are born with English as your first language, I find these things to be the basics of knowledge, but not everyone feels that way.

That's okay, there entitled to they're opinion. (See what it does? Hurts the brain doesn't it?)

Accepting something, in this case, is to come to understand the way it is, and sometimes this can be difficult and humbling. Not always though! At some point in your childhood you may have come to the realization that you can not, in fact, defy gravity and fly like Superman (I still hold out for this one - and caused my mother countless heart palpitations as I threw myself off of our garage roof trying to fly over and over again). This would be "accepting" the law of gravity and our inability to manipulate it. Maybe you've come to accept that at 5'6" your chances of being recruited by the NBA are quite slim. These are all called "acceptions". (I know, I know, what about Spud Webb? He would be the exception to the rule.)

Well, getting back to Parkinson's, there may be some acceptions you will have to make, and as I said these can be difficult and humbling, but not always.

First, your aspirations of being a successful brain surgeon are out the window. (SHOOT!) Nobody is going to want Sir Shakes-a-lot cutting into their original home network. I joke because this doesn't apply to most of us, but it's a serious game changer for a few so my heartfelt regards go to them, but at the same time for most of us, whatever.

Photography: A little more common than neurosurgery, might have its challenges but nothing that can't be worked around with the proper equipment. Most cameras, at least for video have a stabilization mechanism built in, and for still photography, there are these fancy things called tripods and remotes.

Fishing fly-tying: may be a challenge, but with some help, still attainable.

World-renowned sniper: definitely not.

Porn star: okay, if this was actually in the cards for you, first of all, congratulations - being a star at anything is commendable. Secondly, you and I both know there are some freaks out there and there is a niche market for everything so you "shake your moneymaker" as they say.

Sales: If you work in sales, this often involves speaking. There are devices you can use to enhance your speech and volume, plus there is always written communication such as e-mail, text, etc. I am currently watching Apple recognize the prevalence of Parkinson's and add assistive options for PD patients. Technology has come a long way and continues to amaze me.

Maintaining your hygiene: this may become tedious. Not to worry, I recommend an electric toothbrush and a bidet for previously mentioned reasons and to make sure you have got both ends covered and clean. (I'll just keep throwing these out there!)

Walking: my current nemesis. You know, I never considered walking to be exercise? I was always active, and certainly wasn't a jock by any measure, but I recreationally participated in just about any activity at one point; when I go to the gym I put in a good effort. I always knew that if my caloric expenditure became so low that I would actually count walking as my "exercise" then I was indeed getting old and out of shape. Now, that was my standard for myself, and it was and still is a tough pill to swallow that I have difficulty walking. And that's no disrespect or judgment towards anyone with a physical disability, this was purely my standard for me. I am in full support of the notion of "the little one may do is still better than the nothing that someone else does". This was one of my humbling challenges to go through. It was even more baffling that in the same day I was teaching flying 360° reverse hooking kicks I would also have trouble making my steps. It really caused me a lot of discouragement! Now, I don't often use the word "hate", it is a negative and energy-draining word but, I can sincerely tell you that I hate(d) my shuffle step. It drove me banana sandwich! But alas, e-scooters! They are just now becoming more mainstream, and I bought one last winter to be more environmentally friendly and more economical for getting back and forth to work from April to November. Coincidental timing or what? It has at the very least alleviated my frustration with walking and added a bit of carefree fun. Plus it folds up and fits in the trunk of the car, so I can take it anywhere and I have a backup plan when the car gets work done or the tires are changed, etc.

You will learn your waves of on/off and use them accordingly. If you're in an "off" phase and you are shaky or weak perhaps not the time to sew a button or change your watch battery. This would be the time to rest, read or watch something. Likewise, when you are "on" don't waste it. Have a plan to be active, be social, or get some to-do's done. It's all about working with your schedule, which will be different for everyone, but do not let it frustrate you as it is mostly out of your control. Learn your patterns of off, on, dyskinesia, dystonia, etc. and you will have an easier time with your daily activities. Your neurologist may have a tracking sheet to monitor these patterns and it will help you with understanding your waves.

At the time of writing this chapter I have been approved for Deep Brain Stimulation surgery. This is like a pacemaker for your brain, an apparent game changer for some Parkinson's patients. It addresses only certain symptoms (fortunately the ones that I have) but not other symptoms (fortunately the ones that I do not have). However, there are a few things that are prohibited once this surgery is done. Scuba diving for example. I have my certification for it and to me, it's the closest I can get to flying; however, the underwater pressure is a potential hazard to the implanted device. The good news is snorkeling is still doable. Skydiving, again I have done it and would do it again in a heartbeat but it is not recommended post-DBS surgery. My kids would like to do it and they want to do it with me, so next month we shall pull off a 10,000-foot jump and check off one of their bucket list items before my surgery. Contact sparring, now this one hits a little close to home as I teach and train Taekwon-Do. Unfortunately, the potential of getting kicked in the head or chest will now have its increased risk of the device getting damaged or dislodged. At my core, I'm not a big fan of getting hit so I will be okay with it, but at the same time that feeling of a high-speed, Mortal Combat-like, exchange of techniques is a rush that I will miss. That is okay though, it is rare for someone my age and rank to still compete, and there are always pattern and board breaking categories to perform in which I quite enjoy. Just this year I received a Canadian bronze medal for pattern competition at the National Championships. My neurosurgeon is in full support of continued training and competition, just no contact sparring, so I will be "hanging up the gloves" as they say.

My point in all of this is that there will be changes, challenges, and acceptions to make, but they can be worked around. With the right attitude there's a solution to each problem, but be patient with yourself and your caregivers. Learn to adjust your sails so you can still move forward in life. Alter what you need to and accept what you can not change. That's life - it is not what happens to you that defines you, it is how you deal with it that defines you.

HEY, SNAP OUT OF IT!

You know, living with Parkinson's can be challenging, but that doesn't mean it has to preoccupy your mind 24/7. It is easy to slip into the survival state of just getting through the day, and I understand that feeling. Sometimes it is just difficult to take a step out of bed without feeling defeated before you even get started. This can wear on you and beat you down. Every once in a while, you need to pull your head out of that slump and SNAP OUT OF IT!

The most exciting time in your life was probably when you were either pursuing a goal or in the midst of fulfilling one and you will want to continue to do this. You MUST do this. Life without hope is energy-draining, and the word "hopeless" really does sum up this emotion. Living without a desire to win at something or achieve something more makes you like a deflated balloon, a soft apple, a limp handshake, or lukewarm soup. When you are INspired you are no longer EXpiring - you can't breathe in and out at the same time. In this case of life's journey, rotten fruit can become fresh again by re-igniting dreams and goals. Get out that bucket list and add to it. Get around a dreamer or goal-setter or go out and enjoy what you enjoy with open eyes/ears to receive new goals and direction.

Over the past while I have been riding the waves of daily medications, side effects, relief, on phases, off phases, eat, sleep, repeat. It's easy to get caught up in the rhythm and have your focus just on the "now", and sometimes there's a need for that - to be present, in the moment. Also, sometimes you need to stick your head above the fog and remember where you were going in the first place. Parkinson's does not have to be a total life derailment, it may have altered or slowed the journey but you are still on the tracks and you can still hit some destinations and objectives.

Recently I was in a restaurant where there appeared to be a large group of about 20, a team of young children, some adults and one older couple seated at the head of the table - seemingly, the grandparents and definitely the common thread of the group. I came to find out that it was the grandfather's 70th birthday and they had all come from across the region to celebrate with him. What caught my attention the most was the 6 grandchildren all gathered around the 70-year-old man after dinner and all of the adults watching and smiling. They were presenting him with an album of some sort filled with precious memories of times shared and passed. This golden image of a man who had clearly earned the love and respect of his offspring and their offspring, surrounded by this joyful group made me well up inside. I don't know how he did it dry-eyed, looking through the album, pointing out each memory or item that was in the gift (which was put together by family members living at different distances by the way). It inspired in me a new dream, and like the Latin meaning of inspire, "to breathe into", it breathed life into me again. I had been so caught up in tracking my daily habits, doing my to-do's, and honestly not looking further than 2-3 months in advance, that I had forgotten to dream-build and set long-term goals. Remember you don't die from Parkinson's, you die with it, which means it's not a death sentence! I understand that when you are quite literally on shaky ground or feel like you are shuffling along on an unstable footing you tend to look straight down to stay balanced. (I count tiles to keep focused when I'm walking in an off-state) When you can, and I recommend the sooner the better, pick your head up and look ahead. Before you got distracted by this diagnosis, you had some dreams to accomplish, didn't you? There were some things that you had not yet accomplished and they are likely still attainable. Even an injured lion wants to roar again.

After dinner, I greeted that 70-year-old man, whom I found out to be named Clarke from Nanoose Bay, BC and thanked him for the inspiring moment. He beamed with gratitude, but I'm not sure who felt more grateful, him or me? Thanks, Mr. Clarke. I hope this book finds you well.

FOR THE MEN AND THEIR TEARS

(This revelation came to me during an annual memorial for my nephew. He was a wonderful young man who died tragically at the young age of 19, leaving an empty and unfillable hole in all of our hearts. It's to him that I give credit and to his mourning parents that I dedicate this message. I love you, Duncan, always have, always will.)

What does it mean to be a man? What does it mean to be a woman? More relevantly, do these things matter? We currently live in an era when the traditional definitions of gender are being constantly challenged and redefined. I am not here to tell you what to believe and what not to believe and I am certainly nobody's judge; unless of course, you degrade a person's value purely based on what they believe - in that case, I would be inclined to judge you all day long, but that leads to a logical paradox for another time.

I am here to propose a thought that may be a bond, a mutually beneficial connection between my generation and the next. I am here to be a maven, calling upon the thought of a traditional stereotype and translating it to a comfortable, perhaps more enlightened position of understanding. A thought that hopefully will empower you, in the long run, as a human being. Having said that, I am a straight white male for which I make no apologies, and nor should you for how you were born or who you choose to be, but you should know the source so you can better understand this message. Naturally, my goal is for good and thus hope it is relatable to as many as possible, to make the world a better place for everyone.

In my own personal journey as a man, I recognize the modern acceptance of men shedding tears not being a sign of weakness, but rather as a sign of being human. We, as a society, understand now that it is emotionally and psychologically healthy to shed and synthesize these emotions; and yet, some men still seem to battle those lingering feelings of internal weakness, vulnerability and embarrassment when emotions are exercised to such an extreme that tears are expelled from the soul. Much like having a choking experience, one's natural reaction is to remove oneself from public view, out of embarrassment, and choke in private - anyone with a medical background will know that this is a great way to die alone. Having lived my share of extreme joyous moments in life as well as sad and emotionally traumatic times, I submit to you a slightly different perspective on the tear-jerking response that we encounter, a perspective that may be more palatable for "a man" to take.

First of all, we need to recognize that tears can come from both good and bad experiences, and, secondly, can result from both emotional and physical causes. If you've ever been punched in the nose, eaten a hot pepper, or even just chopped onions you have teared up. These are not signs of weakness or strength, they are human physiological responses. The nasal passage is connected to the eyes via the tear ducts and when the nose is struck the lacrimal fluid that normally flows through the nose gets restricted and thus overflows through the tear ducts. Onions release a sulfuric acid which irritates the eyes causing them to tear. Peppers have capsaicin which binds to pain receptors in our mouths causing our nose and eyes to water. These are all commonly known and accepted biological responses. However, when it comes to emotional causes, both positive and negative, our judgment comes into question. Why is that? Is your sense of judgment called into question when you chop onions? No. Why then would it be called into judgment during different stimuli over which you also don't have control? It is due to a lack of understanding or perhaps comfortability with this cause-and-effect scenario, and this may likely source in the level of maturity. It isn't the presence of tears that makes someone feel less "manly", but instead the acceptance of whether the level of stimulation from the event is justifiable in revealing the so-called "control" over the response. In other words, it's your confidence that this response is warranted that in fact reveals your level of maturity which is mistakenly interpreted as feelings of masculinity, not the tears themselves. So really, at the core of all this emotional upheaval is one's confidence that the tears are justified and this level of confidence is what is disabling, not the tears. In fact, if it was clear to everyone that the tears were justified, one would be less apprehensive to shed them. See the difference?

I submit to you, as a 48 years young man, a proud father of 2 functional aspiring young adults, an accomplished black belt, an honourary member of Mensa, and a happily loved husband who is comfortable in his own skin, having been tempered with multiple life-traumatizing/enriching events and surrounded by high functioning pillars of success, that there are, in fact, certain undeniable cause and effect scenarios over which you have no control. They are as factual as the existence of your face and as the old saying goes, "It is what it is". We work with what we've got. The sooner you come to terms with this, the sooner you will come to the understanding that your tearful response is justified and thus the more confident you will be in your response - thus more "manly", if you want to call it that. Many books like the famous Man of Steel and Velvet by Aubrey Andelin have tried explaining this notion but, I feel, not from this perspective (even the title of the book evokes a powerful image).

I don't know who needs to hear this message but hopefully, it is helpful. My true desire is that you will not avoid tearful situations, because that would also be denying you the true joys life has to offer. Remember, this physiological response can result from both positive AND negative experiences. Tears are inevitable. My wish for you is simply that you have more joyful experiences that cause you tears than sad ones, AND that you become mature and comfortable with both. Walk proud, keep your chin up, "be a man" and own your responses confidently. This will be your sign of maturity, which bundled with your experiences, will lead you to a more successful and prosperous life.

ADRENALINE RUSH

Demi, our puppy, is our newfound love in the family. She is named because she is 1/2 the size of most dogs. Demi is French for half (demi-tasse, demi glaze, demigod, etc.) She is a wonderful addition to our household. You see I grew up with dogs and I love them. My kids have always wanted a dog but now they are getting older and the idea of getting one was losing its lustre. Knowing how badly they wanted one, getting one AFTER they moved out would seem cruel. My wife, though, grew up on a ranch. "ANIMALS BELONG OUTSIDE and you certainly don't name them." The thought of an animal being inside the house, on the furniture, shedding, peeing and pooping everywhere was ludicrous. She was against the idea from go.

Then one amazing day she sent me a picture of a puppy and asked what I thought of her. Her?? I'm not sexist, I just never thought of having a female dog. I always pictured a boy dog. I mean if you were to charade-act out a dog, you would most likely say, "Here, boy!" or hike a leg to pee, or WAIT, hold on, SUE IS LOOKING AT PUPPIES??! It was a Cockapoo (Cocker Spaniel/Miniature Poodle cross), 1 of 4 in the litter, black and brown with a small patch of white on the chest, 8 weeks old and she looked like a teddy bear. Cockapoos are hypoallergenic, don't shed and are incredibly smart animals. I asked if she was available? She was on Kijiji, a local online garage sale website, and yes, she was available. In fact, the owner could meet us that weekend! She was perfect, and for my wife to have picked her out was a home run hit! We just had to convince the kids. Yeah right! Demi was love at first sight for all of us. The most adorable little furball and she was complete with snuggles, puppy kisses and tiny little puppy moans. Not an aggressive bone in her body and all love. To this day I wonder how she puts up with all of the love she is given, being picked up, snuggled, face-to-face nuzzling, etc. She was quickly woven into our hearts of myself, my wife, my daughter and especially my son. I could tell that she was a key component in boosting my kid's mental health at the time, which has been on my radar, especially since my health challenges have probably played a challenging role. Demi was trained, to the best of our ability, and welcomed in the house, on the chairs, on the bed, even next to "Mrs. Animals-belong-outside". She had stolen our hearts.

At full grown, she reached just shy of 9 pounds, depending on whether she had a haircut or not recently. She maintained her teddy bear appearance and stole the hearts of many in the community.

Walking her was a job for all of us, although admittedly we all did it differently, which is a no-no when you are a parent of a puppy in training. Landon would walk her on and off leash, I would have her on leash but not holding onto it (it just gave me the extra ability to catch her should she not stay close, but gave her that sense of being under control), and my wife and daughter insisted on leash. All methods worked for each of us in their own right.

One night, I was in between teaching Taekwon-Do classes and waiting for the adults to arrive for the final session. I timed my medication to work out with the class times, but by the end of the adults class (8:30pm) I was usually spent. Students were beginning to arrive and I got a call from Landon which was strange because he would usually text. The level of concern in his voice caught my attention. "Demi got scared by a jogger and took off, I thought she would be at home, but she's not and I have no idea where she is."

Now, this can be concerning for any parent of a puppy, but there were a few things to consider here. It was the middle of winter, she's 9 pounds, it was -10°C outside, and we were surrounded by snow and wilderness. Cougars are seen regularly around our neck of the woods. Plus, she was on a leash, which means she could be stuck somewhere on a branch and not able to get free. In addition to that the Apple AirTag that she was equipped with wasn't pinging; which meant she was nowhere near civilization. Landon was distraught at the time, but kept it together. I dropped what I was doing and drove home immediately. By this time, Sue and Tana had arrived from town and were out looking in the neighbourhood. I had ski pants overtop of my dobok pants and a winter coat and we began searching. It had been an hour or two by this time and at her speed that could mean anywhere in a 1-2km distance, although the likelihood was she would be close by, possibly scared. We checked under porches, backyards, the golf course, neighbourhood streets. I was in the car slowly driving with a flashlight and calling her name. I posted on our local Facebook page for the community to watch out for her. She had my number on her tag and if anyone came upon her she was sure to be returned safely.

A few hours went by without success. Tana had covered the resort twice by foot, Landon had exhausted all possibilities he could think of, Sue was in the streets carrying her slipper, one of Demi's favourite things, and there were dozens of community members out searching and it was getting bleak. I knew that every minute that went by in the cold, with predators around, the potential outcome was getting worse and worse. My son carried a mountain of guilt, one that I knew could be challenging for him moving forward. We are all on the verge of tears, fearing the worst. I was resolute, just keep looking. Tana stayed home in case Demi returned, Landon and Sue continued calling and wandering, and I went to our neighbour's house to borrow some snowshoes. We were surrounded by a golf course, which in the winter is wide open areas with clumps of dense forest. Behind our house was a ravine with a rushing creek, which due to a mild winter was still open - yet another potential hazard. I put on the snowshoes, made sure I was dressed warmly, and with a flashlight in hand I went out in the deep snow and dark of night calling Demi's name. This was hour 4 or 5 now, I have been pumping blood over 100bpm for most of the time, just taught 3 classes of TKD, and at the max of my medication, and I was fighting my shuffle-step off - literally telling it to "f*** off" in my mind in between calling for Demi. On the flip side, I had food, wasn't too far away from help if needed, I had my phone so I knew I was trackable, the bears are hibernating and cougars don't attack full-grown adults, often. I figured that I would be ok.

115

I was in and out of the ravine, along the golf course, across the creek, through dense bush for almost an hour. It was getting close to midnight and many of the locals had given up looking, reserving the thought that she would eventually come home on her own. I couldn't go to sleep thinking that she was out in the cold, stuck on a branch and sitting as prey to whatever could be out there. I needed to at least know what happened, although I feared that answer greatly. My adrenaline was still pumping, but after that many hours and with my walking ability, I knew that I looked like a man on his last breaths.

My phone rang, it was Tana. "She pinged on the AirTag 1/2 hour ago!" Of course, how stupid of me! I had stopped checking my AirTag tracker! I was too busy focussing on breathing and stepping, and in snowshoes! I must have walked close enough to her for the AirTag tracker to respond. She was in the ravine behind our house, but by now I was on the other side of the golf course. I hurriedly made tracks back towards our house and halfway there I got a joyous call from Tana, "She's here! She's here! I went out back to look for her and she came running up to me!!" What a relief! My whole soul relaxed, and my whole body shut down. The 4 hours of adrenaline dump was over and it had taken its toll on me. What would normally have taken 1-2 minutes to walk took me a good half an hour. I was spent, but relieved. It was good to find out that if needed my body could still perform, somewhat.

We stayed in as a family the next day, still wearing off the emotional taxing of the previous night's events. Demi learned to use a treadmill for the rest of the week.

Just kidding.

DBS INTERLUDE
BEFORE

Well, the date is set, my bilateral sub-thalamic nucleus Deep Brain Stimulation (or DBS) surgery is in 3 months. As I write this I am both excited for the results and nervous about the procedure.

For those of you who are not familiar with DBS, it is a procedure that is effective at assisting with movement disorders associated with Parkinson's. It is done by inserting two electrodes into the STN part of the brain to stimulate motor movement, thus taking over the role of Levocarb but without the side effects or waves. Once these 2 electrodes are inserted correctly, the battery pack/neurotransmitter is surgically implanted just below the clavicle and the wiring is run sub-dermally down the neck. This little battery pack/neurotransmitter is about the size of a pocket watch and gets changed every 5 years (minor local procedure). The surgery has been reported over the last 10-15 years as a game changer for many who have had it done and I am optimistic it will be the same for me. While the surgeon cannot promise a complete reduction of medication, it stands to reason that there will be some.

The procedure takes about 4-5 hours. I am told I will check into the hospital on day 1, spend the night unmedicated, have surgery/recovery on day 2, and if all things go as planned released on day 3. Following this, there is a 4-6 week recovery period, after which, if there are no infections or complications, I will return to the DBS clinic where they will then turn on the device. There will be some fine-tuning for a few weeks to ensure the device is working properly and at the level I need. If it's working properly I should be in my "on" phase 24/7, which for me is still pretty close to normal. All sounds awesome, right?

Like any surgery, there are risks. In this case, risk of stroke during the surgery, infection after the fact, the surgeon sneezes and I taste peanut butter for the rest of my days, all that stuff. I have never had anyone "look at my wiring" before so I am nervous about the unknown. The brain is such a complex myriad of wonders I speculate as to what may change after such a procedure. Remember I love my life, and would rather have it WITH Parkinson's versus not at all. Also, during the electrode insertion, do you know how they know they have the correct area of the brain? Your verbal response. What?? Yes, you are awake while they do this! They numb the scalp and screw a frame on your head called a "halo". This keeps you still while two holes are drilled into the skull and then the electrodes are inserted! Once confirmation is made of the correct location and frequency, THEN I will be put under while the surgeon implants the wiring and battery pack. It may be a small relief that the brain actually has no pain sensors and of course, they anesthetize your skull, but yeah, THAT!

It's encouraging to know that these physicians and surgeons are elite at what they do, and perhaps a little competitive in that they won't perform such an elective surgery if they aren't confident in its success. Also, this is all this surgeon does and he's done thousands successfully.

This procedure is the next step in my journey with the condition as medication is becoming less effective for me and my waves of "on" time are diminishing. I am currently taking Levocarb every 3 hours, sometimes with an agonist called Amantadine (although I call it Adamantium like the metal lining Wolverine's skeleton in X-Men because it just sounds cooler). After 20-30 minutes my medication kicks in for about 45 minutes. That's not much time for feeling normal. I am still able to maintain my work and teaching of martial arts but I question being able to keep up as a student in my own TKD class and at work I manage many times dependent on the good graces of my colleagues. I am not nearly the star performer that I once was. Remember I once considered feeling "normal" a downgrade; now it's a faint wish.

But, I keep my head up, my eyes focused on the next goal, and I charge on like the knight in Monty Python's The Holy Grail. "It's just a flesh wound!" While I still am ambivalent about the looming surgery, my training in becoming a black belt many years ago reminds me that I am impervious to fear. Not that I don't feel it, but that it doesn't grip me from doing what needs to be done. That it doesn't permeate my soul. That I maintain a spirit of indomitability. I say this now, let's see how I am on game day lying on the gurney.

SUPERPOWER

"Just a walk in the park for a guy like you."

Some comforting words from my friend, Russ. It's truly amazing how words can encourage and inspire. Has someone ever asked you, "if you could have any superpower, what would it be?" For me, it's been clear for years - the ability to always have the right thing to say. Whether it's making someone feel better, understand more, or get what is wanted out of life, I believe this divine skill would be invaluable. Almost like an altruistic, telepathic ability where you can evoke the best response from them with your words, but not by taking over a person's mind. Think about it! I knew this was my true wish when it superseded my desire to fly like Superman. I have always wanted to fly, unassisted. Since as far back as memory serves - I jumped off of rooftops as a child, ran super fast with angled cardboard, prayed, leaped over obstacles - anything to unlock this potential ability to fly. As an adult I have skydived (indoor and outdoor), paraglided, zip-lined, and flown in helicopters and private aircraft - again anything to have me in the air. I love it! You see, when you're young at heart, superpowers are options, not silly fictitious notions. When this concept of the ability to have perfect communication entered my mind, the desire to fly played second fiddle.

My friend Russ had that superpower today, if only briefly, when he asked me about my upcoming surgery. "Just a walk in the park for a guy like you," he replied. I needed that. They were the right words. Thanks, Russ Morrison!

Game day approaches.

FALL FROM GRACE

I was out for a walk with my daughter and talking about life as I often do and enjoy with my kids. My legs were not working well again and it was causing me some frustration. I explained to my daughter that even though my feet just wanted to plant themselves rather than move, surprisingly I had not yet fallen. In almost every neurological appointment I have had with Parkinson's I have been asked if I had fallen. So much so that I asked my wife for an Apple Watch for Christmas, as it detects if you have fallen and calls for help even if you can't. I also live in a snowy environment for the better part of 6 months of the year and I had heard too many stories about that one guy that was out on his deck or rooftop shoveling and had a heart attack and was unable to call for help. What a sad and preventable way to go out. Apple Watch also monitors your heart rate and upon any strange sudden irregularities will, again, alert you and call for medical help, transmit your location and hopefully get help for you ASAP.

Now I was at least somewhat prepared should such a fall or heart failure occur. Fortunately, my balance was quite good and I had been unaffected by the loss of equilibrium that is common with Parkinson's. When I said to my daughter that I had never fallen it was almost as if that thought fluttered up to fate, or whatever you believe in, and reminded said force that this box had not been checked off yet. "Challenge accepted, "said they.

Cut to later that evening: I am at work. The night is going well, very little regression in my condition and it's beginning to quiet down from dinner. It was near the end of dinner service and there were not many guests left. I was transporting a drink from the bar to a table and just as I picked up the service tray my legs began to shut down. I should've known better and asked for someone else to run it. This had become a common practice as of late when there was no way I was stable enough to carry a tray of martinis or an open cup of coffee without the tray looking like there had been an earthquake. Well, the earth began to shake, my feet began to get heavy, but my body insisted on carrying on. It all happened so fast, I rounded the corner of the railing, my steps caught the attention of the nearby table, my feet stut-stut-stuttered and down I went. Like a toddler carrying their juice too fast, I did a Maggie Simpson flat on my face. The tray went forward, the drink flew off of it and I sprawled "OOF!" chest to the ground. Again the restaurant wasn't full, but I was in the middle of it for everyone's viewing pleasure. The room went silent, but at the same time I heard an audible "Ooooh!" and I even think I heard a record scratch as my torso screamed to a halt on the rock-hard tile floor. I was dazed a little, as one would be, taking a hit like that, but fortunately, when an emergency happens my awareness heightens and time slows down for me. I remained still, sensors up.

"I'm on the floor? Check."

"Conscious? Check."

"All systems go? Check."

"Any pain reports? Negative."

"Any broken glass around me? Negative."

"Is it safe to get up? Slowly."

Luckily, a concerned guest was there quickly to help me up, keep me calm and remind me to stand up slowly. Unfortunately, one of my fight or flight responses is a narrowing of vision, (most people are this way, others' widen) so I'm not sure who was around. I was aware that people were around me and were politely dissipating themselves as I righted myself and came to. One person went to get the precautionary WET FLOOR sign, one person guided me for a few steps and I shuffled to the back of the restaurant, stopping to ask one of my colleagues to get a replacement drink to the table. I got to the back and my supervisor met me there, wide-eyed with concern. It's worth stating here, if I haven't already, that my employer and fellow co-workers have been nothing but supportive, professional and accommodating during my time with Parkinson's. Even seasonal workers, without a history together have been amazingly accepting and helpful.

I stood there in a bit of shock, remembering that I had earlier stated to my daughter that I had never fallen. My rationalizing brain kicked in pointing out that I didn't fall, I tripped. One is a loss of balance with no visible cause (thus must be a result of Parkinson's) and the other is a result of something or someone innocently interfering with your stride. I tripped, just like anyone may have when something was in front of their feet. I just happened to have Parkinson's also. And the invisible object that I tripped over was, in fact, my foot.

So there I was sitting in the back of the restaurant in shock and a stunning amount of embarrassment, I might add. I asked my manager, "How much of that has to be reported?" I knew the proper answer: all of it. Abiding by health and safety regulations a legalistic person would have to document the incident - I was now a potential liability. Placing me in subsequent situations without improvement could be a further danger to myself or even to a guest. Human rights and Employment Standards Canada would have a field day with a company that relieved an employee based on a disability that formed while employed with them - especially a 16-year respected one. No, I wouldn't be fired. I would be reassigned to other duties, ones that didn't involve much walking but there's not much money in that. I don't know how much you know about the restaurant industry but a waiter here in North America is generally paid the minimum wage; a god portion of their income comes from gratuities. The government knows this, that's why the wage is kept at minimum. It's not a perfect system but it is a good one. A good server can earn a decent income in a resort town like this one but it's peaks and valleys when it comes to business volumes. I was a supervising lead server, which meant I was paid a bit more all the time, supervising or not, but I had some extra privileges and responsibilities. Contrary to popular belief you do pay taxes on gratuities - you wouldn't survive in the industry for any length of time if the IRS/CRA had anything to say about it. And to my Australian friends, both here and abroad, you are *not* paid a comparable living wage in a non-tipping system, taxed or not.

If the Department's Director got wind of my being a potential liability I could be downgraded to support. I was only 3 weeks away from my DBS surgery and I had to make hay while the sun shined! So I asked my manager, "How much of that has to be reported?" He replied, "I was going to ask you. How much do you want to be reported?" I calmly replied, "None of it. I tripped, it was nobody's fault and I'm alright. No worker's compensation required." He said, "Okay, that's the way it was then." Hallelujah! I was safe, for now. Let's go surgery, you can't come soon enough!

By the way, the Apple Watch never went off.

THE ECONOMY OF GOOD

Newton's 2nd Law of Thermodynamics has fascinated me for years. It is also known as The Law of Entropy and it essentially says that as one goes forward in time, the net entropy (degree of disorder) of any isolated or closed system will always increase (or at a minimum stay the same). This means that anything left alone will not naturally get better, improve or get more organized. A quick example: imagine leaving a toddler alone in a room filled with toys neatly arranged for 20 minutes and see what it looks like when you return? (Okay, maybe don't really do this, but you can imagine the hypothetical result, it wouldn't get tidier!) Need another example? A car left out in the woods over time will age, rust, and decompose. If you leave a Kia sitting out in the elements for 10 years don't expect that nature has turned it into a Mercedes when you return! I've always found this interesting about the theory of evolution, where things have "evolved" or gotten greater over time. There seems to be a great deal of discrepancy here, especially since science calls Newton's concepts LAWS and Darwin's concepts THEORIES. I don't want to digress here too much, but the essential concept to grasp here is that things don't get better when left unattended.

My father always taught me that there was more good in the world than bad, you just have to have an eye for it. He also taught, by his example more than his words, to always put good into the world. Weeds take over a garden if left unattended, buildings collapse if not maintained, machines break down if not serviced, and society degrades if not replenished with good. One of my mentors during my young adulthood had a plaque and it read "All that it takes for the forces of evil to rule the world is for enough good people to do nothing." Now, some would say that this is a spiritual calling, a biblical decree or even Karma. I'm not going to tell you what to believe and this isn't a sermon. Whether you want to believe in a god's approval, the way of the universe or Karma it's completely up to you. I submit then when you put good into the world, that it's now out there, quantitative, measurable and observable, if you've got the right eye for it. This being said, I don't put good into the world because it will come back to me; that's never been my motive. I put good into the world because it makes the world a better place for everyone, including me and my own. The world can be a better place just by your good deeds. Whether it multiplies exponentially like the "Pay It Forward" concept or it just carries on linearly like each person paying for the car behind them in the drive-through. It makes you feel good doing it and makes someone else feel good receiving it - and hopefully inspires them to continue the favour. Don't be confused, that good is out there in the world, bouncing around and leaving its mark, perhaps like the butterfly effect. It's like a drop of coffee in a glass of pure water, you can't take it back out again.

If you think that doing good deeds brings favour with your god, and I would be tempted to agree with you, then there's an economy at hand isn't there? I call it The Economy of Good. When you live your life looking for opportunities to do good for other people, you can't help but be rewarded, but again that shouldn't be the motive.

I have a good friend who is amazing at this and he inspires me to this day. As one of many examples, we were sitting visiting in a coffee shop one time and some elderly ladies walked past the window with their walkers and canes. I saw them out of the corner of my eye but paid no mind and continued our conversation. Corey naturally got up on his feet getting the door for them as they were apparently coming into the coffee shop. I had no idea; he just has an eye for seeing where help might be needed. The ladies beamed with appreciation. He's the guy you want at your till, making you smile, bringing you out of your shell, the guy that'll pour your beer first out of the jug, that will eat the crappy chocolate out of the box because of the two that are left he knows the other one is your favourite. That's good stuff! We work off each other like partners in crime, but he continually schools me. All. The. Time. He feels the same way about me so iron sharpens iron, I guess.

And so I have lived my adult life, as best as I can surrounding myself with great examples hoping to glean from them both their good habits and a character worthy of note. You can't help from benefitting living in an environment surrounded by good people. Unfortunately, the opposite is also true. Those surrounded by ill-intended, mean, selfish people can't help but turn out less than favourable. It's true what your parents may have taught you, that you are a product of your environment. I was told that the person you will be in 5 years depends on the books that you read and the people with whom you associate. (thanks Brad Duncan)

Back to the Economy of Good. If people are earning "their points" doing good deeds and making the world a better place, then someone has to, at some point, play the recipient of said goodness. This I have found, in my journey, is honestly something I need to work on. I can take my kids down the street and plug expired parking meters with coins, or pay for the next person's toll on the highway all day long and receive pure joy out of doing so, but when my account of good deeds becomes high enough to earn reward I have to admit that I become a little uneasy. I wouldn't say I feel undeserving of someone's good turn, but it's along the same line. Right now as I write this chapter, I am weeks away from brain surgery and time off work. Another instructor from over 200 miles away has volunteered to come and teach my martial arts classes so my students don't fall behind because of my medical issue. His dad had Parkinson's and he knew I would be laid up for some time. "No problem, Mr. Oevermann, I've got you covered." My sister-in-law just created a website to raise $1000s to help us cover expenses and people I've never even met before are contributing. A restaurant that I worked at 16 years ago is holding a fundraiser party in my honour to help us out financially. 16 YEARS AGO! My daughter needed a new bed mattress so we bought it and had it shipped to our house, but the local delivery company wouldn't take payment because they wanted to help out the way that they could, "stating you've done a lot for our community, it's time for us to give back". Family and friends messaging from around the globe saying "You've got this! If you need anything, we've got you. And in

the meantime here's what I'm going to do to help you out..."
It's all been so overwhelming that I've been what a friend of
mine calls a "soup sandwich" all week. I could dehydrate
myself with grateful tears for all of the love that my family
and I have received lately. This feeling I have of being not
worthy of it all, I believe is healthy in the sense that it keeps
you humble, but holy smokes has it challenged me to my
core.

And so I've realized something. In the Economy of Good,
there is a time to give what you can into the world in
whichever way you can, and I will live in this zone for the rest
of my days. Sometimes, however, you have to let go and be
the recipient of the goodness so that someone else can "earn
their points". I humbly struggle with this but my heart is
overflowing with gratitude, and you know what this makes
me want to do? Put more good into the world.

THE SOUND OF SILENCE

We've gotten to know each other pretty well so far. I've shared some pretty intimate and open thoughts with you.

I have never been one of those guys who think, "I'm in the bathroom, there's a door separating us, so I can make all the disgusting noises in here that I want and nobody can hear me, right?". And I understand biology, that we're all human and sometimes things have to happen in a bathroom, but trust me, whatever noises escape your lavatorial sanctum while you are in there, you're going to be viewed in a different light for it. Don't think that someone isn't noting what your shoes look like so they can play a little matching game later.

One morning, I woke up from sleeping on the couch. Why I was there isn't important right now. I had just taken my morning medication and it hadn't kicked in yet. You know what had though? My digestive system! As I've explained, the muscular control of a Parky is not the greatest, including those used in retention. So I urgently shuffle step my half-asleep and trembling body to the main floor bathroom. There are 3 bathrooms in our house, one per floor. My first choice would be my ensuite bathroom which has more privacy and a bidet but given the urgency of the situation, my mobility and distance from it that's not going to happen without Mt. Vesuvius happening on the stairs. Downstairs is out of the question for the same reasons, so the main floor bathroom it is. I get to the toilet, sit down and try to relax, again muscles firing, sputtering and misfiring like a spaceship on Star Wars, wounded from battle. You know, one that Watto probably worked on. I am relieved that I made it in time and am about to open the cargo bay doors to drop holy terror and my sweet teenaged daughter emerges from her bedroom and decides to sit down right outside the bathroom door! I hear her and our puppy and I'm sure they are exchanging their usual morning snuggles. My digestive system on the other hand is not feeling so snuggly and comes to such a screeching halt that the pucker factor screams to an all-time high. Now I didn't turn on the fan because it had been making an awful noise in the ceiling lately, one that surely would have woken everyone, and so it was now deathly quiet in the house. There's no TV or radio on, everyone else is asleep, and I am prairie-dogging it as best as I can trying to hold in everything so as not to expose my daughter to the horrible bathroom symphony that is about to take place. I know she's not doing anything wrong, she's just cuddling her puppy because they just woke up. BUT RIGHT OUTSIDE THE BATHROOM DOOR?? NOW??? Ok, I thought, whatever, she doesn't know the rule about creating cover fire or at least space when someone is in the bathroom, so I give her the benefit of the doubt.

"Hi," I calmly text.

"Hello," she replies.

"You know, hanging outside a bathroom door is a little creepy." (This, by the way, is a very subdued understatement as I am squirming to hold Fat Man and Little Boy in with all the energy that I have.)

"I cuddlin my puppy. She on the floor," my daughter responded with modern-day text-like grammar.

"You should take her for a pee and a poop," I texted back. (LIKE RIGHT NOW! I thought it, but I didn't type it.)

"No, she so sleepy"

"She's full. Of pee and poop" (SO AM I, BTW, a bead of sweat forming on my brow)

"Well she's obviously too sleepy to care" (O-M-G!)

As an aside here, there has been a recent history of asking our teenaged daughter to do a task and then being met with face-contorted, grumbling resistance that is so painful to a parent that sometimes you just say in your mind "Fuck it, save the waterboarding, I will do it myself. It's less painful." Can any parents relate?

I cut to the chase, "OK then, could you go away so I can finish going to the bathroom?"

"You make no sense."

"I need to go the bathroom and I don't need an audience."

Her: "MY BAD FOR WANTING TO CUDDLE MY PUPPY AND SHE'S THE ONE LAYING ON THE FLOOR IN FRONT OF THE BATHROOM!!"

I should mention here that my daughter's name on my phone is "Walking Exclamation Point". One might say that she characteristically speaks in large caps.

Oy vay. I can hear her slowly raise herself and carry on somewhere far enough away that I can finally relax and unleash the hounds of hell. And it was a religious experience, let me tell you, an exorcism of the highest regard!

I should have just turned on the fan when I went in there. And now I must go and explain to my daughter the proper etiquette of "bathroom cover fire".

DBS INTERLUDE (PART II)
PRE-GAME SHOW

What is a show without an opening act, right? We are headed to Vancouver, normally a 4 hour drive through a beautiful mountain pass. Today that route might close on account of a winter storm, as it is February. So we will take the alternate route known as the Fraser Canyon. It's like driving the two legs of a triangle rather than the hypotenuse, but it's manageable. 2 Honda Accords hitting the open road, good winter tires, no rush, and all day to get there. My mom was visiting for the surgery and she had originally planned to fly and meet us there but instead decided to drive to us and we would continue from there. Having 5 plus luggage could have been a little cozier than we would like so we opted to take two cars.

Over the previous weeks, my friends, family, and local community raised a sum of money to help with our expenses, for which I am forever indebted. The "givesendgo" website, the private contributions, the fundraiser at my previous employer, well, all made our coming weeks easier to handle than it would have been otherwise. Everywhere we turned there was kindness being offered in our direction. Basically, we had some flexibility to bring a second car and my mother who, even though living 900km away from us and is 30 years my senior, has been with me at every major event in my life (shout out to Moms everywhere). I also felt it helpful to have alternate transportation arranged for my family's back and forth from hotel to hospital, allowing some to visit and some to be at the hotel.

The drive was going to be a bit longer today as the route chosen was the second choice for a reason. Lower altitude, no snow, less reckless drivers but, all in all, should've been only an extra hour. Since we left Kamloops at 10:30am, after dropping off our puppy and seeing my brother (quite possibly, I suspected, for the last time) we were off. However, the weather had different plans for us.

The weather system had snow at higher altitudes, which means what at lower altitudes? Right, rain! Buckets of it! And the wind was still there, boy was it ever! I have never in my life exited a freeway accidentally! I certainly have never seen a bundle of dead branches fly almost sideways into my car. It was horrendous! At one point I pulled over and just sat in the car, hoping somebody might deflate my daughter's saucer-sized eyes and change my shorts. I called ahead to my wife to check in and they were handling it like champions. I told them we would catch up with them but we were going to take some country roads at a slower pace and get there eventually.

At 7:00pm we checked into our downtown hotel, which was still ok but we had tickets for a 7:30pm show just over the bridge. I had booked us into the Improv Theatre for something called theatre sports. Quick plug, if you ever have an evening free in Vancouver, I highly recommend this. You pay less than a movie ticket and you come out sore from laughing at stuff that couldn't have been written or ever again performed. So fun! We needed that, and I needed a cold beer. My friend Bruce and his family joined us which made it more enjoyable. As I previously explained in the Introduction of this book, Bruce had been a good friend since high school and he also had a background in grief counseling. I asked him to be with my family on surgery day so that there was a shoulder for Mom, Sue and the kids, just in case things went sideways. He's a good friend, one who has also been there for many of my major life events. So it was good to connect with him, a little pre-game huddle so-to-speak.

The next morning we had some time to kill before checking in at the hospital so we went and toured the university that my son was planning to attend in the coming fall. He was interested in the film industry and Capilano University had a great amount of resources and a promising program. After that it was back to UBC for my hospital check-in. This was a university hospital, which is a learning environment, also coincidentally next door to the movement disorders clinic where I was diagnosed 5 years previously. We settled in with some gourmet Allen & Wright burgers (A&W to the youngins) and a deck of UNO cards and waited for the resident doctor to come and see us. Dr. Ho, a Chinese-Australian man, was one of Dr. Honey's resident surgeons and he briefed us on the procedure and filled in any gaps or unknowns that we had. My daughter was especially anxious which I honestly couldn't help with. Other than the fact that the odds were in our favour of the surgery being a success, there was an undeniable chance of something going wrong - and I don't make promises I can't keep. When your little girl looks up at you and says "promise me you won't die" and you are not 100% sure of that.....well, let's just say it was difficult.

Hours went by, games were played and it eventually came to the point where we were just prolonging the inevitable. We said goodnight to each other, not knowing if it would be our last. I had decided that since the surgery was scheduled for 6:30am and the hotel was 20 minutes away on good roads, they should return after the surgery to see me, rather than coming by beforehand. It was snowing outside which meant the city basically shuts down. (Vancouver is a very proud Canadian city, but when it snows they lose their minds.) It was with mixed emotions we said our goodnights and went on with our evenings; my family to their hotel and me to my semi-private room. And now we wait.

DBS INTERLUDE (PART III)
GAME DAY

"Ryan, Ryan, good morning," Nancy whispered, "it's 6:30 and they'll be here soon to get you."

I had apparently slept well, as I always did when I didn't wear my transdermal Rotigotine patch. My eyes were glued shut from a good night's rest in a reclined position of the new hospital bed. These things would recline, bend at the knee, go up and down, charge your mobile device, massage your calves, do your laundry, etc. As I mentioned I was at UBC, which is a learning facility as well as a hospital. This means that it is clean, well-funded and not overrun with much of the transient downtown scene. I know that risks sounding uppity but when you are there for brain surgery cleanliness and calmness are environmental traits you value. Although my insurance had covered a private room, there wasn't one available at the time, so it was me and William, a 78-year-old Chinese man with dementia. His son said that he had been there since before Christmas and it was now the end of February. William struck me as a misunderstood man, being poked and prodded every 3-4 hours to eat, poop, pee, take his pills, repeat, and at times seeming a bit obstinate - but you go through that day in, day out for over 2 months and see how you are! I'm a very cooperative and grateful patient, but people are not always at their best in these situations. God Bless nurses!

Well, it was "game day", and the moment had come. The thought of this surgery had pretty much occupied my mind for the previous 4-5 months. I knew that it was the next logical step for me in my journey with Parkinson's, so that decision was pretty easy to make as there were no other viable options that I was aware of. Was it safe? Yes, 95% chance of a positive result.   Can I be real with you? (yeah, I'm asking now like an idiot!) That 5% was on my mind 24/7 and quite honestly scared the daylights out of me. Someone was about to look at my wiring under the hood which had never been done before. Sure, you and I sneeze unexpectedly and that's no big deal. Dr. Honey does and it is Sarah McLachlan time! Ever get an unexpected shiver or twitch?

As I have stated many times, I am an optimist. Sometimes, so much so that it drives my wife nuts, but I think deep down inside she leans on it and appreciates it (I hope). However I also had to be pragmatic, as I have people depending on me and who love me. I sat up many tear-filled nights writing to my wife, my children, my parents, my friends, my students, my mentors...all "from the grave". In the event that something did go wrong, I wanted things taken care of. Quite honestly, half of me did not think I would return from this, so I HAD TO PREPARE for that. Even though I expected the best, it would be absolutely foolish and irresponsible of me to not plan for the worst. I made sure life insurance policies were in place, codes, passwords, keys, were to be made available to my newly widowed wife, with full instructions on how to handle my inevitability. That was all easy street - try writing your final words to your children. Then imagine them having to read it after you're gone. Many, many, many tissue boxes - I should have bought stock in Kleenex. The whole time, my dog sat there with the look on her face that said, "What the heck is wrong with you, man?! Get it together!"

Anyhow my family had left the hospital the night before after hours of UNO cards to return to their hotel in the downtown core. I felt it would be easier if they weren't there in the morning, especially at that time, in the winter snow. My wife of course was willing to be there if I felt I needed her, but to be honest I knew this day would be easier to handle if

147

it was just me and MY emotions. I can keep those in check, but everyone else's in addition to that, would be a different story. My "little girl" was 17 at the time, but her and I agreed long ago that no matter how old, tall, wise or strong she may get she will always be "my little girl", and likewise I would always be her "daddy". And "we dealed on that." several times. She had been especially fretting over the surgery, not totally confident in its success (much I had been but I had, and never would share those doubts with her - well I guess until now). The visit that evening with the surgeon's resident, Dr. Ho, helped some, but nobody could completely console my daughter. I can only imagine what my wife went through with the kids that night on the way back to the hotel. My son was a pillar of stability and typical humour, as he has been for both of my ladies over the years. He always knows how to cheer them up; he just has that magic about him.

And here was Nancy, who I would later learn was my liaison between myself and the nurses and doctors. She was my advocate, my right hand and I will never forget her kindness or her peaceful blue eyes, since that was all I could see of her face. She was there to make sure I got to the correct place for the procedure. Upon her suggestion, I got up to pee. I had no medication since the evening before, so I was a little rough on the take-off but I made it for one world-record urination. Afterward she handed me the pre-op towelettes to wipe myself down (for the surgery pre-op, not from the pee, I hope) and then I was back on the bed and off to the MRI department for a quick photo shoot. Eric was the first nurse (of many) to come along and say hello. Since I had checked in, the entire team had been amazing. Every nurse introduced themselves and explained what they were there to do and that means a lot! They treated you like a person, a human being, not just a patient or a number, even though I understand that professionally they have to be careful with that fine line to remain objective in their roles. It made me proud of our medical system, the one we "don't pay" for. You see there is a gross misconception that our medical system is free. Right, and so your physician bought his Mercedes with what then, tacos?? We pay for it, it isn't free, but not nearly to what it costs, as it is highly subsidized. This surgery, for example, costs around $120,000 CAD all said and done, but I haven't seen a bill and my premiums didn't go up. It made me proud to be Canadian. I can tell you that everyone here in Canada has a horror story about our medical system; but, I can also tell you that there are not many places in the world where you would be catered to like I was. I was treated like a person, not an animal or subject - and there is a significant difference.

Eric was going to drive me down to the MRI pre-op room

149

where they were going to fit me for the next step - the halo. As we approached I recognized Dr. Honey, despite his mask, he had that cool presence and eye contact. Until then I had only met some of his team face to face, but not him. It felt a little ominous as we were down in the basement it felt like, but it was early and I was still fuzzy, so it didn't seem to bother me. I thought it was better to stay calm and fuzzy than get wound-up and wiggly. You know when you first wake up, that funk that you're in? When you are so dopey and relaxed you could just go back to sleep? I just thought I would hang out there for as long as I could. Dr. Honey re-explained what was going to happen: they would numb the skin and screw 4 tiny screws in my cranium to fit the halo, and then fit the MRI attachment to it. Kind of like a birdcage on a base, and I was the bird. The base looked like Ironman's neckpiece without the helmet on. This was meant to keep my head still and not carry any tremors into the MRI machine as it scanned my brain. The screws being driven into the skull was one of the parts I was not looking forward to. As they did this my eyes were closed and I could feel someone's hands on my feet. It was calming, even though the pressure on the skull was increasing with every turn of the screw as they locked it down. I can't say it was painful per se, just uncomfortable as it squeezed your head essentially.

Once the cage was on they slid me "like a pizza", if I remember Dr. Honey's words correctly, onto a different bed for the MRI. Dr. Honey was directing every move of each nurse and orderly with great mastery. With my head movement now restricted I really had to rely on my hearing to know what was going on. As I was being slid into the tube, I remembered that I was claustrophobic and had forgotten my anti-anxiety pill. Whatever, I thought (thanks morning funk). Basically, my brain had a quick chat with itself: "Should we freak out and make a scene making the day rougher for all of us or should we remain calm and relaxed?" Well, I was already calm and relaxed so this was the better option. This "conversation" all happened faster than the speed of thought by the way. The tech said I was in there for 4 minutes, but it felt like 1-2. If you've never had an MRI before, first of all, what planet have you been living on, and second have you ever been to a Daft Punk'd concert?? Out I came and back into the hallway where everyone had been. I'm sure they had all been doing something, but what, I didn't know. The birdcage was removed leaving just the lower base on my head - screws still in place.

If I remember correctly Dr. Honey drove, or at least escorted, me to the pre-op waiting area. Nancy said it would be probably up to an hour there in pre-op, as they were waiting for the operating room to be prepped and ready. Even though it was now 7:30AM, I was actually Dr. Honey's second operation that day. So glad he had a warm-up to work out the morning coffee jitters, although after many years I'm sure this was just another day for him. Alejandro came in and took my information for consent and Operating Room admitting. His job was to make sure my body was A) the correct one, B) was consenting to this procedure and C) was ready to enter a sterile environment. Nothing that could carry bacteria into the OR was permitted. Unfortunately, my wedding ring wasn't coming off (it hasn't for 20+ years) so we had to tape it up. My underwear, pants, gown, everything was removed. Alejandro was nice, a little green at his job, but nice. He was clearly new and was checking off each box as he went. Alejandro had one cool toy, a heating blanket. Not just any heating blanket but an air sac that I controlled and circulated air throughout keeping me warm. At some point, I was fitted with calf massagers for circulation during surgery to help avoid blood clots. So there I was sitting in the pre-op hallway, calf massager, air sac, Iron Man cage. Alejandro gave me a Tylenol and an antacid and fitted me with a tracker on my wrist. I asked him where he thought I was going to go with a bird cage on my head and no pants. He laughed. I'll never forget this halo on my head either. For some reason, the bar came right across the front of the chin and I didn't realize until then that your chin slides forward when you smile. This being across the chin I wasn't able to smile the whole time I was wearing it. And that's weird for me!

Next was the nasal decolonization. Alejandro gave me a sponge on a stick with some interactive blue dye and I was to wipe it all up in the nasal passage on both sides. "Get every corner that I could," he said. Then he gave me 2 tiny straw-like flashlights to stick up my nose, which combined with the blue dye killed any bacteria on board. Once that was finished, I had to ask Alejandro if I could stand up as my ass was killing me! It could have been my lack of medication or just the angle of the bed but I had to stretch.

At this point, John, the anesthesiologist, came and introduced himself. I love these guys, the chemist with his bag of tricks who sit perched at the end of the gurney on his phone just waiting for the chance to play God. I told him I wasn't a big fan of pain, and he had my permission to keep it away from me as much as needed. We agreed on the plan and then were informed that the operating room was finally ready. They gave me one last chance to pee but I didn't have to. "Let's roll," I said and we were off.

Now I forget who was driving the table this time, it might have been Eric, but he wheeled my table in backward to the operating room, which I thought strange at first, but looking back I understand. You just don't need a patient who is about do go through such a procedure seeing all of the torture devices, I mean, ahem, surgical tools. Dr. Honey introduced me to the team, including Austrian Neurosurgical Fellow, Dr. Schmidt and of course, the other Neurosurgical Fellow, Dr. Ho, whom I met the evening previous. In this particular area of expertise, a "Fellow" is a neurosurgeon who spends an extra year learning a specific technique - in this case DBS. There was one area of the room, due to my limited range of movement that I couldn't see, however. It didn't bother me at all, the more I saw of the room probably the worse off I would be. Looking back and knowing that this was a hospital on university grounds, I'm pretty sure there were more people there than was necessary for the operation. As long as nobody lost any junior mints we were going to be okay. Now, where are my Seinfeld fans?

They began the procedure with Dr. Honey speaking clearly about what was about to happen for the hospital records sort of like the Captain's Logue you would hear at the beginning of a Star Trek episode. Then they began with a head scrub that took so long I was beginning to wonder if that was how he was going in, scrubbing. They gave me some more anesthetic to numb my scalp and we waited. Nancy fixed the TV screen in front of me with a live feed of a Hawaiian beach. John mentioned that the day before was funny because a pigeon had been the highlight of the show in front of the camera. I didn't watch it much, I was in my happy place between consciousness and sleep. I was alert, aware, and yet ironically dopey and calm, like when you first wake up in bed - similar to a Zen state.

Dr. Honey then began shaving parts of my head. I should point out here that the man clearly commanded a lot of respect in his field, being the only physician doing this procedure in all of the province and having a 5-year waitlist. Students come from all over the world just to study with/under him. He is the professor and head of neurosurgery at the University of British Columbia, an MD with a Doctorate in Philosophy, and of course, an active surgeon. However, I can vouch, without a shadow of a doubt he does NOT make his money from his haircutting skills because, DAYUM, it did not look good after.

By this time, the numbing was to have settled in and they re-affirmed me that I should feel no pain at all and should I feel anything at all that I was to speak up. "Do you mean like the needle that's touching my forehead right now?" I calmly asked. There was a small murmuring and bustling of needles and then about 3-4 pricks on my scalp as some anesthetic ran down the side of my head. "Good, just making sure!" Now they could begin.

I took a moment to remind John, the anesthesiologist, that I was still there and that he should be "Johnny on the spot with the juice", in the event I needed him. Hey, he had a job to do and it wasn't on his phone. I know, it was just another day at the office for him and I did need him calm, but I also needed him alert and ready.

As Dr. Honey had explained to me previously, the drilling of the skull was both painless and surreal. Using a high-speed drill at 70,000rpm bone literally turns to dust. I don't know how to describe it. It sounded much like being at the dentist when they bore out a cavity and yet you are also half-expecting it to be like in Robocop when everything could just go blank any second. He drilled for about 30 long seconds per side if I recall. I remember praying incessantly, but also being "a duck on the water" as they call it - outside seeming calm, stoic and cool but under the surface very busy. As it was happening, there was the hand again on mine, calming me and soothing my spirit. Then the drilling stopped, and he said "that was the worst of it, Ryan, the rest is easy stuff". With that, I either dozed off or it was just really quiet in the room for a bit. You know when your eyes are closed, time goes by, and you lose track of time, space and reality? It felt like that. I mean, there was no measuring device like a clock, traffic or windows, just sheer peace as I laid there - and enjoyed the relief of surviving what most would be terrified of! The skilled and steady hands were back there planting the leads and doing their work and there was very little noise if any. I just pictured the "silence" sign hanging up and everyone actually obeying it. I should mention again, despite the mental adventure here, as Dr. Honey promised there was no pain at all! The brain has no pain sensors, and they were so gentle I didn't feel a thing.

"Okay let's test the left side," Dr. Honey said. Nancy, under Dr. Honey's direction as he was teaching someone else about the frequencies, took her cue. She articulated my wrist, a common neurological test, had me focus on her finger side to side and told me to say out loud "4-5-6". This was repeated several times on each side. I mentioned that I didn't notice any difference but she did and it was ok. I wasn't sure what I was supposed to feel anyhow. On the final test, Dr. Honey reminded me if I felt anything unique to let him know. It was just then I felt something.

"What was it?"

"I don't know."

"Is it gone now?"

"Yes. I'm not sure how to explain it. It was that feeling you get when you get nauseated and your mouth waters and you're about to throw up," I elaborated.

"Okay," he said. "Is it back again?"

"YUP!" I yelled back.

"Okay, that's good, we're all finished."

Instantly the feeling was gone.

And that was the end of the first half. They sewed me up and got the halo off of me.

Nancy was still there beside me. The whole time she was there. I realized at the MRI she was the one holding my feet when they put in the screws. When they drilled into my head, it was her hand holding mine. I had barely realized it but other than the pre-op screening, she was there the entire time, watching and comforting me from start to finish. I looked up at her and said, "I can never thank you enough for your gentle touch. It meant a lot to me." And it did. I knew this because when I tried explaining it all to my family later, I broke down. Such a simple thing, being there for someone. I know some would say that Dr. Honey was the star that day, and maybe that's true. Some would say I was on centre stage that day. To me it was Nancy. She was my hero.

DBS INTERLUDE (PART IV)
HALF TIME

The stitches were in, the "halo" was off, no more screws in my cranium and it was time for a breather. Dr. Honey and his team wrapped up and cleared out while John got ready for the next show. I could see him mixing his cocktails and syringes. He handed me the mask and said, "We're just going to prime your body with some oxygen first and then it's sleepy time." To my immediate right was a med student, and behind me was his instructor. The student was holding the mask but there was no seal so I was just kind of breathing mixed air - tight here has to be a seal, I knew that much. The nurse instructor guided his hand overtop of the mask and said, "You've got to seal it off so push firmly" and he did, but as soon as she let go of his hand the seal was broken again. I looked up at him and he didn't notice the wheezing of air escaping. I saw John busy doing something off to the side so I tried to free my hands to help. Now, medical teams don't typically care for a "patient assist" during surgery, even pre-op, in this case, so I expected some hesitation. I reached up real slowly pulled the mask tight to my face and sealed it on. "Yes, like that," the instructor said.

"Ryan, Ryan, you're all finished. My name is Nicole. Your wife has been called and they are waiting for you."

Confused? Yes, so was I! I had a couple killer lines ready for John what seemed liked a few minutes ago, "Hey what's for lunch?" or "what's the drink special today?" and I never got to use any of it! I looked down and there was a device in my chest and I couldn't feel much else. Nicole asked me the usual questions: name, date, where I was ("in bed" was apparently the incorrect answer, by the way). She asked if the catheter was still in, to which I replied, "WHAT??" and lifted the blanket to check, but no catheter. Call me "crazy" but I am not a big fan of a tube up the wiener, asleep or not. "They must have removed it already," she said. I guess I did have to pee! Sorry, John!

After all was kosher, I was wheeled out of recovery, down the hall towards my room where I passed by the waiting lounge where Bruce and my family were eagerly waiting. It was like crossing the finish line of a looooong race and I MADE IT! They were a sight for sore eyes. I was a little afraid of my daughter hurting me with her Daddy hugs, but she was

160

good. They said, "So how was it?" and I replied, "Well, I know Kung fu." (Matrix shout out anyone??)

Everyone stood around my bed smiling and watching me and then I saw my wife's face. She was exhausted! Relieved but exhausted. I said, "Why don't you guys head back to the hotel and chill. I'm going to rest here for a while and then I will see you later." And so they went back and all rested up while I cleaned up my room and caught up on some e-mails. Apparently, Grandma took the kids for dinner and Sue went to sleep. She needed it.

The next morning, Dr. Honey and Dr. Ho showed up with about half a dozen others. He looked me over and said, "That was one of the easiest surgeries I have done, everything that possibly could go wrong, went right." You see, if half the number of people prayed for me that said they were going to that day, I just pictured God saying, "Alright enough already! I get it, you like this guy!" Dr. Honey continued, "Any questions for me before we send you off?" I couldn't resist, I had to ask it. "Yes," I said, "where did you learn to cut hair?" The room responded with half sheepish laughter, as Dr. Honey is quite revered in his area of expertise and well respected. I hope I didn't embarrass him too much.

After they left, I could hear William, the Chinese gentleman in the next bed. His son, God bless him, was trying to get him to take his medication and he didn't want to. I felt sorry for William and later that day Sue caught me staring at him, but she couldn't see the tears welling up in my eyes. She whispered, "Ryan, you shouldn't stare." I guess I was staring and I know that I don't like it, but I felt that I understood William. I saw him. You see it's very easy to become exhausted with 24/7 care. Every 3-4 hours somebody is wiping your ass, telling you what to do, what to take, what you shouldn't do, what you shouldn't take, etc. And I saw a man that was all there on the inside, but he was tired. He wanted to check out of his OWN hospital, not just the UBC one, but his family wasn't ready for that yet. In fact, they gave us the credit for the extended care home calling them that morning as a spot had "opened up". It's funny what we celebrate, isn't it? I mean there's a reason the spot opened up! Anyhow, I saw William for what he was. A man who had lived his best 78 years and was ready to move on. I'm not sure if he ever got to the extended care facility, but wherever he is I hope he's happy again.

DBS INTERLUDE (PART V)
POST GAME WRAP-UP

The trip home was broken up into 2 days. Again, it's only a 4-hour drive if the mountain pass is open and clear but since the weather was still poor and we had a generous offer to stay at a place along the way we thought that avoiding the snow one more night would be smart. It was again, one of those random acts of kindness from a "friend of a friend" sort of thing for which we are forever grateful. I mean, can you explain it? A person that you have never met, from out of the blue, messages you and says, "hey, we have an extra home, we're not using it for the next while and here is the code!" It really is amazing the good in people that exists out there!

We pulled into the mall parking lot in the early afternoon about an hour after we checked out of the hospital. My hair was in fine form as I had mentioned, with patchwork bandages over the front of my skull. I'm sure at some point pre-surgery someone had recommended a hat for the ride home, but I don't remember it. Sue pulled the keys out of the ignition, looked at me and said, "Wanna borrow my hoodie?" I replied that I was okay. A second later my son was opening the car door asking, "Hey Dadda, want to borrow my hoodie?" "No thanks," I replied, "but apparently we need to find a hat store in the mall and fast!"

We walked into the first outdoor store and I boldly asked, "Where are your hats? We need to fix this!" I said, circling my head. We found a North Face hat to replace one that I had lost a few weeks earlier looking for our puppy in the woods. My wife must have noticed the look on the clerks' faces and explained that I had just been through surgery.

We wandered the mall for an hour or so and then headed on down the road for dinner before hitting the family fun park along the highway. It was one of those places your dad always said "no no, we'll stop there on the way home" and you knew you never would, because who actually stops on the way home?? Then we went to the condo and we called it a night. The next morning the mountain highway had closed and so we ended up going back the way we came down, the Fraser Canyon. There was a fair amount of construction which made the trip even more arduous. I drove the last half as I was feeling fine and not under any medication. I mentioned to my wife that we should stop and gas up and then do some grocery shopping to avoid the need to drive back into town the next day. She was too exhausted to think about it so I sent her and the kids home and I did some shopping. Looking back it would have been wise for someone to stay with me, but c'est la vie.

It bothered my wife to no end that I had more energy coming out of brain surgery than any normal person would. "I don't know how but since I do," I explained, "I'm going to use it." I mean, I wasn't going to lie, I felt great! No fuzziness, no festinating steps, no tremor, basically no Parkinson's! The next few days were the same. I would be walking through the village and people would be looking at me like they had seen a ghost! "Didn't you just have surgery?" they would ask, "Shouldn't you be at home, resting??" I can't explain it, I felt like I could have gotten the surgery done on the weekend and back to work Monday morning. I could hardly remember to take my medication, I felt so good! It wasn't going to last, I knew that, so I enjoyed it while I could. Ahhhhh, honeymoon...

HURRY UP AND WAIT

The waiting period between my DBS surgery could not have felt longer. I was off work, not teaching classes, and had to remain inactive. This was not my strong suit. I survived and thrived through CoVid because I was able to be active and I had a huge to-do list (which I totally crushed). At that time it was new, we had never had a nearly universal break like we did during 2020. You want me to what?? Stay home with my family, my favourite people, play games, watch movies, and work on my own personal to-do list with little-to-no agenda? Just stay home!! Oh, and we're going to pay you not to work. Economically for the world, the pandemic was not good and in many ways we're still paying for it, but I loved it! You see, type "A" personalities always have a to-do list, and sometimes this to-do list gets stale because there are projects on there that if you were to complete, life would pass you by, and we don't care for that at all! However, with CoVid, the whole world paused. This meant I could take my feet out of the pedals of life, get off the bike and look around, and not miss out on anything! I spanked my to-do list, pulverizing project after project, but also had time to inner-reflect, spend quality time with my family, watch EVERY episode of Cheers and Night Court, edit a book for a friend, make a cookbook for my kids, experiment making 10+ cheesecakes, begin to write a legacy book for my kids which will come out after this one, and for the first time in years do my taxes on of time! I realized I could wake up when I wanted to, go to sleep when I was tired, and start a new project whenever my heart desired because I didn't have that nagging feeling of having to be somewhere at a certain time. To me, it was very freeing. Now I realize not everyone felt that way, so I didn't brag about it much, but I was happy.

This time off was different. The world hadn't paused. My family still had their places to be and things to do, so I had to occupy my time. Oh, but "don't you dare go skiing, or lift anything heavy, because that wouldn't look right since you're supposed to be recovering from surgery. And no heavy lifting or home renovation projects." Don't you know I used to be Superman??! No, I was to sit down, lay low, and recover for 50 long days.

Thankfully, I had this book to finish and so here we are. Plus, Mario Kart, lots of Mario Kart with the family - a little deal with the kids to enjoy the moment, even during dark times. You see, in life, tough times are expected and you must learn to smell the roses along the way. This surely was a test for me and the lack of activity drove me nuts.

MOTHERF***IN' PINEAPPLES

My recovery, as I was saying, was not so good, mentally. It was a real struggle for me and there were many sad days. You see, I was not like some Parkys, afflicted with depression or much anxiety (even though I did take a very small dose of clonazepam most nights to ensure and extend my sleep) and since activity is the only thing that has been proven effective in neuroprotection, Inactivity was not my friend. My shuffle step turned into freezing, crutches were used at one point, and my speech and dexterity became so weak and mitigated that many days I just would sit, like that one grandparent at a family gathering, just watching people enjoy their lives moving around and walking and talking. Contrary to what it appeared like, everything was still going on inside my head as usual, but due to my muscles not working correctly, my engagement in life was limited to a depressing level. Ever been there? Being trapped inside a trembling statue, watching life go on but not able to engage in it? Frustrating doesn't begin to describe it. I hated it, and you know how much I dislike that word.

One spring day, the sun was out so I wanted to be out in it. My wife was home from work and the dog needed to be walked. I was on crutches that day since my legs weren't performing as they should. My speech was so weak and cotton-mouthed that communication wasn't very effective. I kept thinking, "I know these words were being sent from my brain to my mouth clearly, but someone isn't holding up their end of the bargain here because they aren't coming out clearly like I hear them in my head!" It didn't help that my wife's hearing was also going at the time - oh the fun that was. Anyhow this one day we went on a short walk around the still-frozen golf course pond. It was a paved path by our house maybe 1km in circumference and somewhat icy in patches. While on the walk our puppy, who was on a leash, got excited to meet a dog that was coming at us (i.e. not on a leash). If your pucker factor just went up right there your instinct serves you well. The general guideline in our community is to walk your dog on a leash if there are people or other dogs around. Some dogs/people are just not dog-friendly, which I don't understand but accept. I mean, how can you not like your species' best friend?? Anyhow, I don't have much of a problem if your dog is unleashed, as long as he isn't a threat to anyone or anything. I was a few steps ahead as it was easier to not walk beside my wife at the time with a puppy, a leash and her on the walkway and me on crutches. The bigger dog approached and lunged at our puppy biting her and causing a high-pitched yelp and sending our puppy cowering at my wife's feet. I was mitigated in my reaction and speechless, as my wife secured our dog and the other one carried on with its owner. Not a word from the other owner, no apology, no empathetic reaction, nothing, just eye contact and walking on. My wife stared in shock and horror as if to say, "Did that just happen?!"

We carried on home, although because of the frustration and anxiety from the situation on both of us, I had to say to Sue, "Hey, my hobbled steps can't keep up with your pissed-off pace." She realized that her totally justified negativity was punishing me in trying to keep up with her while in an "off" state, and she slowed her gait.

Now I said this path was around a pond, so as you can imagine, this can cause you to meet up with the same people now and again. Sure enough, as we approached our house 10 minutes later, I saw the same lady and her dog walking up the stairs to the pathway. This time thankfully, her dog was leashed, however, having just arrived at the literal edge of our unfenced yard, ours had been unleashed to cross the to the front door. I saw trouble brewing so I hobbled down the stairs quickly to head our puppy off and keep her in the yard, when my daughter came to the door. "Thank God," I thought, "able-bodied help!" Sue remained up on the path to protect our puppy from Cujo. My adrenaline and anxiety were kicking in, which when your body doesn't respond well is like flooding an engine, and that's what I probably sounded like when I spoke to my daughter. I was all tied up and unable to move or speak clearly or quick enough. I tried desperately to get my daughter's urgent attention and ask for her help retrieving our puppy, but my words were all jammed up. All she could do was hear both parents trying to yell at her, so she stormed back inside spewing off verbally. Now, had it been me in her position and I understood the whole situation AND I wasn't in full "Parky mode" I would have sock-footedly raced across the icy yard and lunged to save our puppy. Did I mention, my daughter's nickname in my phone was "The Walking Exclamation Point"? So, she's going off, louder than I can compete with, Sue is calling for help over what is cataclysmically about to happen, stomp stomp stomp, goes my daughter, demanding an explanation in the middle of chaos. My wife was able to retrieve Demi and bring her to safety. Cujo's owner, again, no words, nothing - I can only assume she was either mute, foreign or equally in shock.

We got inside and everyone had a chance to cool their jets. I realized something. There will undoubtedly be times when you can't explain everything at the moment, your mouth/body won't keep up with your brain and action will be necessary for someone's safety. This, mixed with the absolute notion that I support that "compliance does not require comprehension" leads me to believe that we need a word or a cue that is A) easy to remember, B) natural to communicate, C) will arrest a person's attention, and D) most importantly say, "Hey, I know that there is a lot more going on here than you are currently aware of and I deeply apologize for my lack of time or ability to sufficiently explain everything to get you on my side right now, BUT, would you be willing to kindly shut the fuck up and do something urgently and I will explain everything to you afterward? This will undoubtedly be in all of our best interests."

I know, it seems obvious, we all need this type of safe word. I was so excited about this idea as it could've been implemented MANY times for me thus far as a father, even pre-Parkinson's. Tana suggested using the word "pineapples" as a cue, which is nice but I wasn't sure I would remember it and it seemed a little subdued for urgent circumstances. What word would I use if I was so flustered, so frustrated and in desperate need of help? What word would I use? And then it hit me. In the heat of a frustrated and penultimate moment, only one word would effortlessly and appropriately slip out of my mouth: motherfucker.

Don't judge, maybe it's the Samuel L. Jackson in me.

And so it was, from that day henceforth, either pineapples or motherfucker, or motherfucking pineapples, that if these words were uttered in any way, it would arrest our attention and launch us into action. Questions to be asked afterward. Now, I can only hope that my final words will not be "motherfucking pineapples"!

A LITTLE MEANS A LOT

Perhaps this chapter could be intertwined with another (Riding Shotgun, for example) but it bears repeating. My philosophy is that if you find yourself in a position where you are able to help out someone with a difficulty, you should, and almost need to. It's just a good-natured way to be. It makes you feel good, the recipient is grateful and any onlookers may be inspired to follow suit, and thus the world is a better place. You would be so surprised how little you would have to do in the case of helping a Parky.

On a daily basis, I have difficulty with a variety of very simple things. Tying up trash bags, screwing on lids (you know when you screw on a lid, oftentimes you back-thread it slightly to catch the thread and then continue to close it? Since I've had Parkinson's EVERY lid has to be back-threaded +90% of the way, I kid you not.) Stuff just aggravates you more. Your jump shots will be just short of

175

making it, closing the refrigerator door will be just shy of successful, opening a produce bag in the grocery store, pulling one card out of your wallet but not all of them, all of these seemingly basic things can become very annoying. Watch for these things, and without trying to take over, offer assistance when you can. It'll be subtle, the cues, but oh so appreciated!

Those who do not suffer from Parkinson's may take for granted these basic abilities. I know that when I'm in an "on" phase I do. Walking to the door, wrapping a gift, prepping food, stirring a pot - all easy things for most people. These things can be difficult for a Parkinson's patient in an "off" phase. Just be aware of it.

It's having the eyes to identify when or where help may be needed. My vision has definitely expanded to recognize when a helping hand might be needed, and it oftentimes doesn't take much effort. A little can mean a lot!

WHAT WOULD THEY THINK

I had been debating what chapter would finalize this book. I try to leave things on a positive note. Like a good movie, you can be taken through the dregs of life emotionally as long as at the end you're taken out and dusted off with the dénouement of resolution. Plus, I just like happy endings to a story.

We are told frequently in life that we shouldn't care what other people think, yet almost in the same breath, we are told how to present ourselves for a job interview. Don't worry about how you dance and sing, and then you watch AGT where they literally judge each performance out loud. Life can be very confusing! To be clear I think you SHOULD care what others think, but you should care what important, relevant, and competent people think. This may coincide with your priority list, or vertical alignment, as it's called (spiritual advisor, boss, spouse, etc.) but I will get to that in a minute.

Today I find myself post-surgery, waiting for my device to

be turned on in the weeks to come, tired of waiting, laying low, relaxing out of fear of what someone else would think if I were active. They say that exercise is the only proven method of neuroprotection for Parkinson's so the more exercise the better. However, after surgery, they tell you to take it easy and don't over-exert yourself as you may hinder recovery. Currently, if I am in my "on" phase I have felt ready for exercise from day 1 (okay, maybe day 2), however, my "off" phases have become more predominant because I am not as active as I usually am. So it's a very frustrating dilemma. If I am seen being active are people going to doubt the severity of the situation?? I have been blessed, as I said, with tremendous support from our local community, but still, are people going to question the hindrance I am living? I am a victim of my own ambition and positive attitude sometimes.

"Didn't you just have brain surgery?? Shouldn't you be at home resting?"

"How dare he go to the gym while off work and on sick leave."

What would so and so think if they saw me? Would they question my need for time off? I know every 30 minutes my ability to walk successfully will be in question, but they may not see that.

I know that my employer can flag my resort pass to see if

it has been used or not - what would someone think if they knew I was skiing, staying active and exercising, when I "should" be at home recuperating like a good boy. This difference between what people perceive and what you experience can really send you into a loop. You see, people may see slivers of your life, only you experience 100% of it. Think about it, you're there for almost every moment of your existence. I would venture a guess that you know more about yourself than anyone else. You do the best you can and hope that people see enough of the real you to get a good picture, but again do you care what they think? If your child tells you that the kids at school were picking on them and calling them names, how would you coach them? What would you say to them?

Clearly, there are times when what someone else thinks IS important. If you work in customer service there are things you can wear/do that will put relatability in your favour. Certain colours, styles, etc. to appeal to the general public and certain ones don't. If you work in sales, this definitely matters. The famous book Dressed For Success, says that people often make a pre-judgment of you based on things as little as your footwear and your watch. This may be antiquated a little, but it begs the question, are first impressions important? I maintain that they are. People will tell you that you shouldn't

179

judge a book by its cover. That's true, you shouldn't, but let me ask you, what usually initiates your picking up of a particular book? The cover. Yes, the hook, the first impression! It matters. Do you see the potential hypocrisy here?

How much should you care what people think? This will depend on the impact that person may have on your life and how much that means to you. This is called your vertical alignment. If you are spiritually inclined, top of the list would be your maker or god. Everything should be acceptable in the eyes of the one you are devoted to. Next of course would be your spouse or significant other. Since you've intertwined your life with theirs, they should have some influence on how you are seen. From there on it could be your family, your coach or mentor, your boss, etc. Notice that all of these are ranked in order of importance to you and the possible relevance to them and your future.

I have found that when people get inspired to implement change in their lives they get up to about 99°C (211°F for the old schoolers), just shy of boiling, because it may involve working hard but let's do it at a comfortable pace, shall we? Most will push themselves in a workout to get a bit of a sweat, but not exhaust themselves because they still have to do stuff for the rest of the day. People have trouble losing weight because you have to burn a certain number of calories away BEFORE you start burning your fat storage. But when the chips are down and you've got "what would so and so think" wrapped all around you like plastic wrap confining you to a claustrophobic state of stagnation, your blood will start to boil and a beast will awaken - it's game time.

You'll have to forgive me here, but we're about to tune into my inside voice, my head, my self-talk. I teach competitively that it's ok to be a little on the arrogant side as long as it A) stays in your head and B) is only shown by your results. Sometimes you have to give yourself a little pep talk to get your game on. And let me point something out to you: if life has been so nice to you that you don't know this already, again I apologize, but as I'm sure most of you know already LIFE IS GOING TO KICK YOU LIKE A MF! (to steal a David Gogginism). There will come a point in your life that enough is enough and you start proverbially swinging. You'll have your Michael Douglas moment from Falling Down. You will hit your boiling point and I'll ask you at that moment: Would you give a good goddamn what someone would think if.....? Fuck em! This is where the champion inside you and your overdrive will all kick in and you'll move! You'll get to a point where you start swinging, like a fighter fighting for his life and you won't give a rat's ass what someone else thinks. You might say something like, "You picked the wrong guy Parkinson's. You've pushed it too far. I am not backing down and I sure as hell am not backing up! I've got the eye of the stinking tiger in me because I'm fast enough, I'm strong enough, I'm young enough, I'm determined enough, I'm burning up and ready to kick your antiquated, archaic ass!"

You give yourself a little pep talk like this each day, and watch what happens.

Life is worth fighting for, so go shake it up!

Until next time friends...

ACKNOWLEDGMENTS

No man is an island; we are indeed products of our environment and those with we surround ourselves. These are people that have poured into my life and influenced me along the way and I thank them deeply for their contributions, either to me or to this book:

Worldwide Group, LLC

Ingo & Jean Oevermann

International Taekwon-Do Federation

*John C. Maxwell (inspired Sometimes You

Win, Sometimes You Learn)

Personal Mentors

David K. Duncan (RIP)

Corey Solomonson

Michael Barker

Andrew Lipsett

Murray Bishop

Derek Strokon

Brian and Barbara Finch (AUS)

Greg Clark

THANKS TO MY MEDICAL TEAM

Dr. Harold Stefanyk MD

Dr. Jennifer Takahashi MD

Dr. Chris Honey MD, DPhil, FRCPC, FACS

       Prof. & Head, Div. of Neurosurgery, UBC

The entire DBS Team in Vancouver

   http://drhoney.org/

   Special Mention: Nancy RN, BSN

ABOUT THE AUTHOR

Ryan lives with his wife and kids in a beautiful mountain resort in Canada. His skills in customer service, martial arts, conflict management, leadership communication skills, humour, and of course, his experience with Parkinson's come together in this book. His sincere hope is that this compilation of stories will enlighten and may even educate those affected by Parkinson's and leave them with a more optimistic view on life.